All Good Gifts

Crafts for Christian Gift-Giving

Marilyn Todd Hagans

paulist press  *new york/ramsey*

Library of Congress
Catalog Card Number: 82-62924

ISBN: 0-8091-2543-9

Published by Paulist Press
545 Island Road, Ramsey, N.J. 07446

Printed and bound in the
United States of America

DEDICATION

To Daniel Bahrenburg, whose baptism was the catalyst; to the All Saints family, the nourishing soil; to Peggy Mathauer, who makes real the ideas; and to my mother and father, who taught me about love and the joy of creation.

CONTENTS

I. Introduction

"Yahweh, what variety you have created..."

Psalm 104:24

In the Christian community we are often torn between the commercialism surrounding gift-giving and our very real desire to give with love. Halloween is a secular holiday, and All Souls' Day is lost; Christmas advertising begins as soon as Halloween is over. All weddings are in June, and Easter is a time for quantities of shellac-covered candy. Insidiously we find ourselves succumbing and counting out our gifts in terms of money: a five-dollar gift for this one, a twenty-dollar gift for that one. Magazines even offer us "100 gifts for under $100!" neatly divided into categories by amount.

This book is for those who would like to give of themselves, within a faith context. Many crafts are mentioned in the Bible, particularly in the later chapters of Exodus or in 2 Chronicles. To work at these crafts, or to work in the materials that the Bible names, is to operate out of the heritage of our faith. Attach a card with a quotation pertaining to the medium in which you have worked, and you have given a "Christian gift."

Both gifts you make and gifts you buy can be transformed by adding symbols and emblems from the Bible, from Christian history, or from legend. Suggestions throughout the book are intended to be adaptable. Emblems and motifs may be reduced, enlarged, or combined with others, and used with gifts other than those suggested.

Wander through fabric departments, getting the "feel" of materials that will go together, or go well with a season, a particular holiday, or a special person. Do the same in lumber stores, and even hardware stores. Look on beaches or in the woods for stones, driftwood, sticks and shells. If you have a camera, take pictures of branches or trees, or arrangements of plants you can't bring home with you; then trace your photographs. Or use slide film, project slides onto paper, and draw around them to make patterns. Make your photographs into picture books, or have them enlarged as posters. As part of our stewardship of the earth's resources, waste as little as possible. Look at everything before you throw it out, to see if it can be turned into a Christian gift.

If you say, "Well, I can sew (or paint, or embroider, or . . .) but I can't *design!*" think again. If you see a picture you would like to put on something, trace the outline, reduce or enlarge it if you wish, and transfer it. Remember: it doesn't have to look exactly the way the original did. A rainbow has seven colors, but you can make one with three or four. You can make it in bold colors or pastels, use it by itself, or combine it with boats, birds, flowers, animals, or people.

Read the Bible with an eye to discovering specific plants, animals, garments, foods, and artifacts of Bible times—you will find far more than are covered in this book. Listen for legends, customs and traditions wherever you go; our faith is rich with them. Once you have begun making Christian gifts, you will notice motifs and ideas almost everywhere you look. Encyclopedias of the Bible, atlases of the Holy Land, books on heraldry and symbolism, and children's picture books are all good sources of ideas.

This book is divided according to types of gifts rather than according to types of crafts or by holidays or occasions. Often we think of gifts in terms of people and their needs and interests. (Let's see: something for Barbara's kitchen because she loves to cook; a cover for the gardening book I'm giving Bob; a special nightshirt for Brian's birthday; a hand-lettered book of prayers for Molly to take to college—and a laundry bag with a dove—even laundry can be a peaceful task.)

Throughout the book there are patterns and ideas which will work well in a variety of media and for many purposes. If you're interested in doing a household gift then turn to that section, but also page through the other sections for some additional symbols, patterns and ideas. Be sure to read the "General Directions" which follow this introduction before beginning any of the projects.

ALL GOOD GIFTS has been designed and written to be an idea-starter and a springboard for your own creativity and originality. A Christian gift is a personal thing given by you to someone you love—a joy to make and a joy to receive.

GENERAL DIRECTIONS, TECHNIQUES AND HINTS

Tools to Keep on Hand

Scissors (two pairs: one for paper, one for fabric; plus pinking shears if you wish)

Iron and ironing surface (a turkish towel on a table or counter top works just fine. Roll up one or two magazines tightly, then roll a hand-size turkish towel around them and fasten with large safety pins: good for small curved seams)

Pencils and a pencil sharpener (a small hand-held metal one is sufficient)

Ballpoint pens

Metal-edge ruler

Cloth measuring tape

Craft knives and saws (one or two of each)

Jigsaw or coping saw

Protractor, compass

Screwdrivers and an assortment of screws

Hammer

Paper punch

Needles (assorted sizes, including embroidery and crewel)

Straight pins

Materials to Keep on Hand

Assorted paper for cards and gift tags

Newspaper and grocery bags

Thread, embroidery floss, crewel yarn, macrame cord

Tracing paper, graph paper, carbon paper

Craft glue and flat toothpicks or paperclips to spread it

Instant decoupage medium (such as "Mod-podge")

Permanent felt-tip markers

Liquid embroidery (assorted colors)

Candle and crayon scraps

Fabric scraps

A box or bag of wood scraps

A box for saving interesting containers (bottles, boxes, anything that looks as though it would be interesting combined with something else)

ALWAYS READ PROJECT DIRECTIONS from beginning to end before starting the project. Be sure you have all materials on hand at the outset.

ALWAYS READ LABELS carefully before purchasing materials, to be sure you have the appropriate materials for your job.

TO AVOID WASTING GLUE: tear a strip of brown paper bag about 1½" wide and 4" to 5" long. Roll it around your finger and glue the loose end. Then pour a small puddle of glue on a 3" square of brown paper, set the rolled cup you have made in the puddle, and let glue dry. If you fill the paper cup with glue, it will not dry out as you work (or even overnight, if it is full). Use flat toothpicks or straightened paper clips for spreading glue over small surfaces, popsicle or craft sticks for larger surfaces.

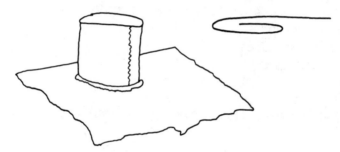

SEWING WITH LEATHER: buy special leather needles. They are available both for hand and machine sewing. When sewing with synthetic leathers, use ballpoint needles.

PAINTING WOODEN ITEMS: be sure to use a primer paint first. Do *not* use primer if you are going to stain or varnish natural wood. Felt-tip markers will soak in and blur on soft woods unless wood is primed.

DECOUPAGE: Glossy papers, such as are used in many magazines, work better than soft or newsprint-type papers.

FABRIC: washable fabrics should be washed (and ironed if necessary) before you start to work with them. Wash and dry at whatever temperature is recommended.

WHEN MAKING GARMENTS, toys or decorations from fabric, iron as you go. Ironing is as much the key to success as the sewing itself.

IRON-ON BONDING: There are two types. One is completely fusible ("Perky-bond," "Stitch-witchery"), so that if placed between two pieces of fabric and steam-ironed, it will join them together. The other is bonded on one side only, and can be ironed to the back of fabric you wish to stiffen (especially in order to embroider details). Be careful not to confuse the two, or you will have a sticky iron.

TO TRANSFER A PATTERN:

a. First trace the pattern, using onionskin or tracing paper and a sharp soft-lead pencil. Or project a slide onto white paper, keeping the projector at a distance that gives you the size you want, and draw around the outline.

b. Transfer to fabric by placing a sheet of carbon paper or dressmaker's carbon, color side down, on fabric. Lay traced pattern on top.

The surface on which you are working should be hard. You may wish to use pins or weights to keep the pattern from slipping during transfer. Draw over the traced design with a hard-lead pencil or ballpoint pen. If you are using the pattern for embroidery, you will cover all carbon markings with thread or yarn. If you are using the pattern for appliqué, you may prefer to cut out the traced design, or transfer it to newspaper or one of the thin pressed fabrics used for making dress patterns, then pin to fabric and cut out.

c. Transfer to wood or paper using carbon paper. Or cut out the pattern and draw around it with pencil or chalk. You may wish to transfer the pattern to thin cardboard, such as shirt board, which will hold its shape as you draw around it and can usually be used several times.

d. To reduce or enlarge a pattern: transfer pattern to graph paper. Determine the size of the pattern you need. On scrap paper (shelf paper, grocery bags or newspaper will work), divide into the *same number of squares* the pattern covers on graph paper. Then, one square at a time, copy the original pattern in its reduced or enlarged form.

ADAPTING DESIGNS

One emblem or pattern may be traced from the book and used at that size, or it may be enlarged or reduced.

One emblem may be transferred to *cloth* and used in appliquéd or embroidered crafts; it may be cut double, stitched, and stuffed for toys, pillows or ornaments.

It may be transferred to *wood*, then painted, stained, or woodburned, as well as cut to shape, and used for blocks and boxes, bookends, birdhouses or feeders, and plaques.

On *paper*, an emblem may be drawn or painted, colored with crayons, felt markers, or pastels. A shape cut from glossy paper can be decoupaged onto wood; a shape from contact paper becomes a decal for notebooks, jars, boxes, glass, metal, and plastic containers. Either drawings or decals can be incorporated into calendars, bookmarks, recipe or prayer cards, books, and stationery.

See illustration for examples—then, throughout the book, think: "How else can I use that?"

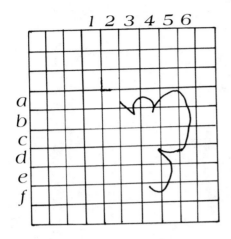

To reduce or enlarge
any pattern—
     make a grid
over pattern or a
tracing of it
     —make a
smaller or larger
grid
     —copy one
square at a time

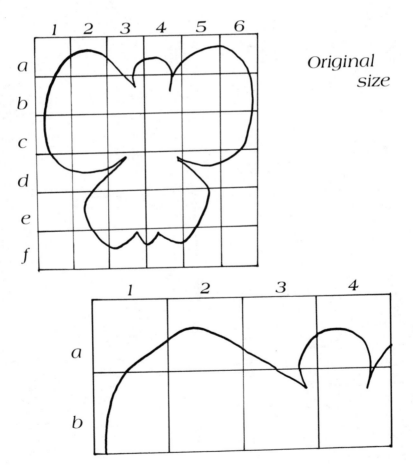

Original
     size

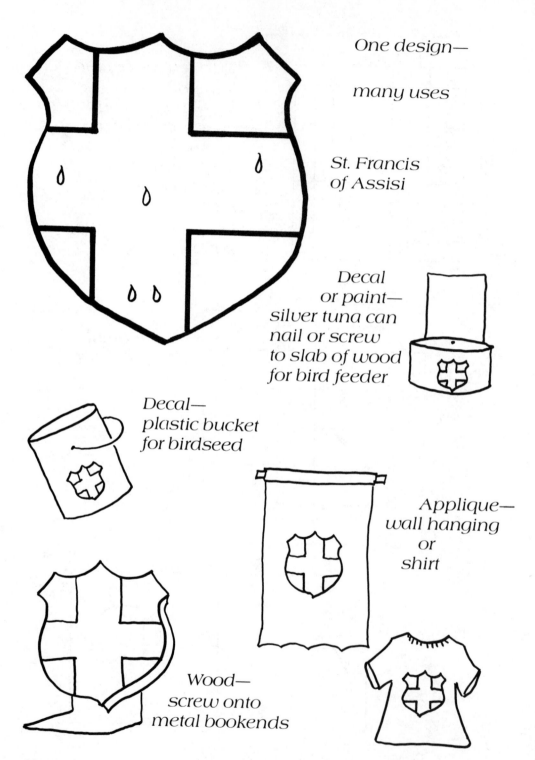

One design—

many uses

St. Francis
of Assisi

Decal
or paint—
silver tuna can
nail or screw
to slab of wood
for bird feeder

Decal—
plastic bucket
for birdseed

Applique—
wall hanging
or
shirt

Wood—
screw onto
metal bookends

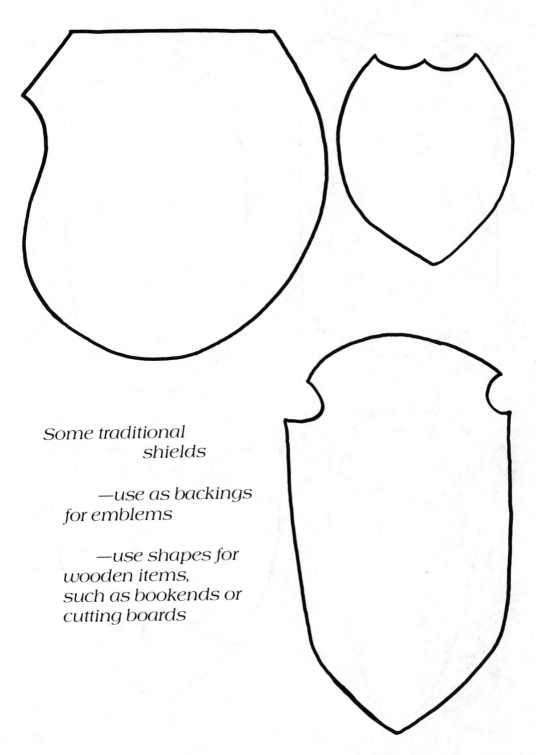

Some traditional
    shields

    —use as backings
for emblems

    —use shapes for
wooden items,
such as bookends or
cutting boards

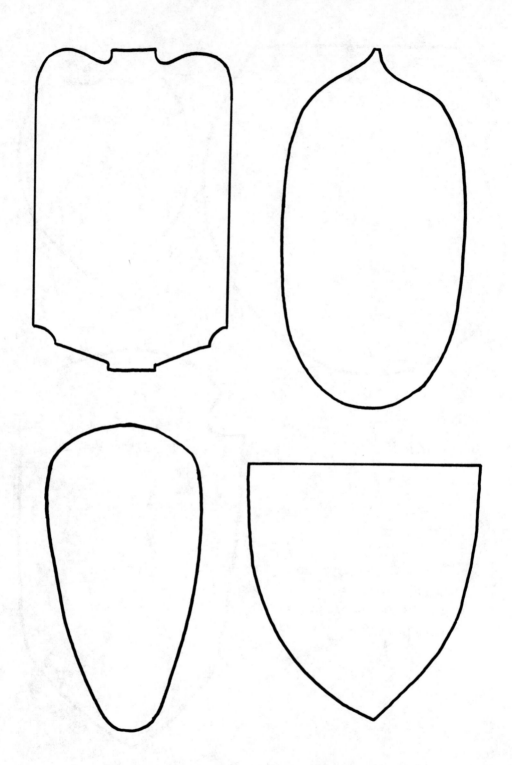

AABCDEFGHIJKKLMM
NNOPQRRSSTUVWXYZ

abcdefgh h ijk klmnnopq
rrrsstuvwwxyyz

AABCDEFGHIJKL
MMNNOPQRSTU
VWXYZ

Alphabets
for writing or embroidery

ABCDEF
GHIJKL
MNOPQ
RSTUV
WXYZ

Alphabet for felt, applique, large markers

18

II. For Books

*"Now your word is a lamp to my feet,
a light on my path."*

Psalm 119:105

BOOK COVERS

Materials:

Sturdy fabric such as denim or corduroy; or synthetic suede or leather.

Amount of fabric depends on size of book to be covered. Cut to height of book plus ½", width of book (including spine) plus 6" to 6½".

Fabric for appliqué; fusible interfacing and bonding. Embroidery materials if desired.

Instructions:

Stitch ⅛" hem on long edges, ⅛" to ¼" hem on narrow edges.

Attach appliqué fabric to fusible interfacing and cut out appliqué; embroider detail if desired.

Place book cover around book, folding flaps to inside. Lay out appliqué and check placement; mark or pin to cover. Remove cover from book and attach appliqué with fusible bonding; stitch if desired.

Fold 2½" of each narrow end toward center. Stitch clear around book cover, ⅛" from edges and folds, taking one diagonal stitch at each corner.

Alternate instructions:

For synthetic suede, cut end pockets off—2½" at each end. Lay right sides together and stitch (hem along top will be created when you turn flaps right side out). Top stitch along top and bottom of cover. This will give a sharper edge than folding flap under, and may be more suitable for paperbacks.

Book Cover Designs

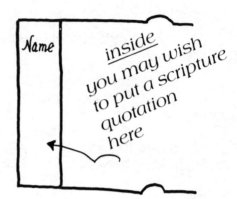

Lamp—symbolic of wisdom,
knowledge:
graduation, birthday, confirmation

Shamrock—the Trinity
St. Patrick's Day, March birthday

Celtic or Ionic
cross: any time

Baptism

Easter

Pentecost

Christmas

BOOKMARKS

<u>Materials:</u>

Fabric, ribbon, synthetic suede or leather, purchased braid; stiff paper or thin cardboard; envelopes.

<u>Instructions:</u>

Variety is limited only by your energy and imagination. Basic types of bookmarks are long—to fit between pages; slotted—to clip over tops of pages; and corner bookmarks (see illustration).

A plain fabric bookmark may be appliquéd or embroidered; paper or cardboard bookmarks may be decorated with drawings or stickers (purchased or made from contact paper).

Make slotted bookmarks from heavy paper, such as card stock, or thin cardboard. Reinforce tops of slits with tape or glued-on paper. Cut slot with craft knife (or with scissors after starting cut with a knife).

Corner bookmark—can be made from paper, stiff fabric, or leatherette. Cut two identical triangles, with the edge to be open opposite the 90-degree angle. Glue or sew together. Designs can be sewed or bonded to one or both triangles. A quick corner bookmark is made by cutting a corner off an envelope.

Fabric or paper bookmark

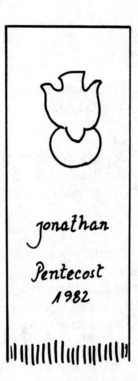

jonathan

Pentecost
1982

Corner bookmark

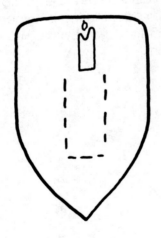

Slotted bookmark

—cut along dotted lines

BOOKENDS

<u>Materials:</u>

Purchased plain metal bookends (or old leftover ones)
Scrap lumber pieces, at least 6" × 6"
Jigsaw or coping saw
Drill
Screws to fasten bookend to wood
Paint, stain, varnish or decoupage medium, as desired; or
carving knives or woodburning needle

<u>Instructions:</u>

Cut two pieces of wood into a square, rectangle, or shield shape. Sand, then decorate: carve or woodburn an emblem; use primer paint, then paint an emblem; cut a picture or shape from glossy paper and decoupage. If you are using a carved or woodburned emblem, you may wish to use walnut or cherry, about 3/4" thick, and finish with a hand-rubbed oil or wax finish.

Drill two holes in the back of wood and through metal uprights of bookend. Put screws through bookend into wood.

<u>Alternate Instructions:</u>

Thin plywood or thick cardboard may be cut to shape and covered with fabric, using polyester stuffing between fabric and backing; glue down edges of fabric on back; glue emblem to bookend with contact cement.

—back view

Tablets of the Law

The Apostle Thomas

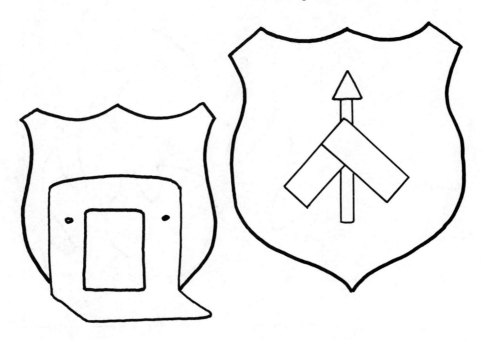

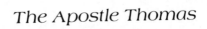

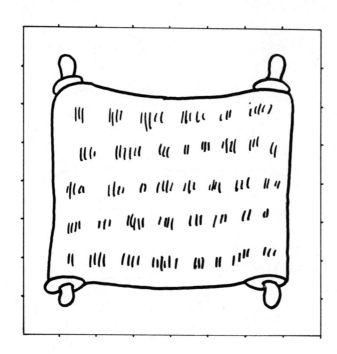

Scroll—
the word
of God

Pentecost

III.   For Carrying

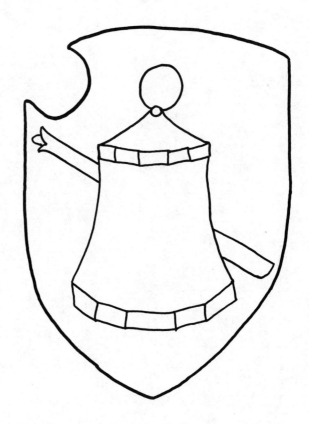

*"Everyone has his own burden
to carry."*

Galatians 6:5

TOTES, BAGS, CARRIERS

Tote bags, wallets, glasses cases, garment and laundry bags, briefcases, bookbags, backpacks, duffles—all these and more, in heavy fabric or synthetic suedes, are perennial favorites. There are several commercial patterns available, most of which offer patterns for three to a dozen items in one envelope. Thus, here you will find directions for only a few simple carriers. To transform the gift, use a symbol for the occasion, for the person, or for a meaningful idea. Make an appliqué of a compatible fabric, and glue, bond or sew to the carrier.

BASIC TOTE BAG

This can be made in any size you wish—tall and narrow for knitting needles, short and wide to serve as a briefcase, smaller for children's lunches or overnights, or a relatively standard size for use as a bookbag or purse.

Materials:

Heavy fabric, such as denim or canvas (lighter weights can be used for bags that will not be carrying books or heavy items). 30" by 13" will give a finished bag of about 12" by 14". Web strap material or additional matching fabric for straps. Thread, sewing machine, fabric for appliqué, fusible bonding.

Instructions:

Turn under $\frac{1}{4}$" on narrow ends of fabric, or stitch on seam binding. Then, turn down a $\frac{3}{4}$" hem, wrong sides together, and stitch.

Cut out appliqué. Fold bag as it will look when finished; place appliqué; stitch in place or attach with fusible bonding. If the bag is likely to be washed frequently, the appliqué should be sewn on. Straps may be added at this point or after bag is stitched together at sides.

To make straps of matching or contrasting fabric, use a piece 3" wide by 18" long. It is easiest to fold the bag and loop a tape measure for the approximate handle size you want. Remember to allow an extra inch on either end of the strap where it will attach to the bag. Fold and press ¼" hem on the long sides of straps. Fold strap together lengthwise, wrong sides together, so that one crease comes almost but not quite to the other. Pin, press, and sew together with either straight or zig-zag stitch.

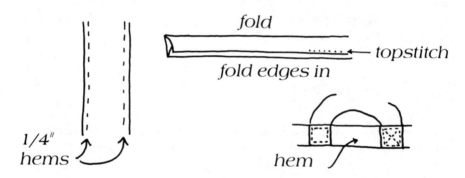

fold

topstitch

fold edges in

1/4" hems

hem

Place ends of one strap over hem about 3" to 3½" from sides of bag. (Straps may be added either inside or outside bag; if outside, a fabric strap will need a small hem at either end to prevent fraying.) Pin strap in place perpendicular to hem. Stitch a square, then an X to join each end of strap to bag. Repeat with second strap.

Right sides together, stitch up sides of bag, using a ⅜" to ½" seam allowance. Double stitch or zig-zag for added strength.

If you wish to give the bag a bottom, grasp a corner and match the side seam with the imaginary fold line of the center bottom. Stitch across this triangle perpendicular to side seam and 1" to 2" from the corner. Repeat for other corner.

Turn bag right side out. Fill it with more gifts if you wish, and give it.

stitch across corner

side seam— match to center bottom

ZIPPER BAG

This bag, too, can be made in many sizes, used for anything from cosmetics to papers and books. Whatever size you choose to make, cut fabric 1" longer than zipper size.

Materials:

(For a 10" × 14" portfolio)
½ yard fabric: canvas, denim, corduroy, or other sturdy fabric; a 14" zipper.

Instructions:

Cut two pieces of fabric, 11" × 15".

Press ¼" hem on long side of each piece.

Lay creased edge of one piece along zipper. Zipper should be facing up, and fabric should be right side up.

Top stitch fabric to zipper, using zipper foot.

Repeat with other piece of fabric.

At this point, make appliqué, place and bond or stitch it to bag.

Turn bag inside out (right sides together) and stitch the two ends and bottom. Trim corners diagonally and turn bag right side out.

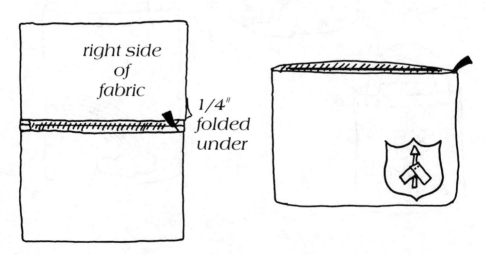

right side of fabric

1/4" folded under

STRING BAG

Fishermen since the beginning of recorded time have whiled away the hours after their nets were repaired by continuing to knot scraps of line into useful and decorative objects. Since several of the apostles were fishermen, perhaps a knotted bag would be a fitting reminder of them.

Materials:

18 strands of soft, sturdy cotton string, 36" long each. (You may vary length for different sized bags.)

Instructions:

Hold all strands together and tie at midpoint, then fold at the tie. You now have 36 strings.

Take any two strands and knot together 2" from point where they join: a square knot is easiest.

Knot the rest of the strands, two by two, until you have eighteen knots.

Lay out on table, spreading out the eighteen double strands in a circle—or hang from a hook.

Take one strand and knot it to a strand from the adjacent pair, 2" from previous knot; continue all around.

Continue knotting, separating strands each time, until you have ten rows of knots.

Divide remaining strands into two groups; divide each group into three parts and braid; tie braids together near ends to form handle.

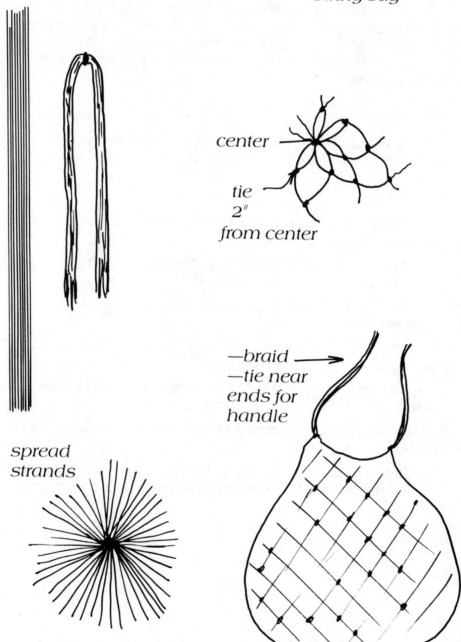

String bag

center

tie
2″
from center

—braid →
—tie near
ends for
handle

spread
strands

IV. For Decoration

"Gates, raise your arches,
rise, you ancient doors,
let the King of Glory in."

Psalm 24:7

HANGINGS

DOOR HANGINGS

A door hanging may be used to celebrate a holiday, a season, or a Christian welcome on the other side of the door.

Materials:

    Upholstery webbing (light brown with red stripes running down either side; available at fabric departments and upholstery or furniture establishments)

    Brass clip-on cafe rings: two or three per hanging

    Thick craft yarn or macrame cord (or other ribbon or yarn of your choice)

    Felt or other sturdy fabric for emblems

    Craft glue

Instructions:

Cut each piece of webbing 8″ to 24″ long, depending on design you choose.

Cut fabric appliqués, lay out for spacing and eye appeal, glue down. For added wear, you may wish to sew the fabric to the backing, although if hangings are packed away carefully in tissue paper, the emblems should stay in place for several seasons, and can be reglued if they come loose.

Attach two cafe rings to top of red stripes, and one ring to center bottom. Run a length of yarn through top rings, tie in bow. The length of the yarn will depend on how much loop you want between the top of the hanging and the nail or cuphook from which it is hung: probably 12″ to 24″.

You may also put a single cafe ring at top and use less cord; if desired, attach yarn to bottom ring as well, and tie in a bow.

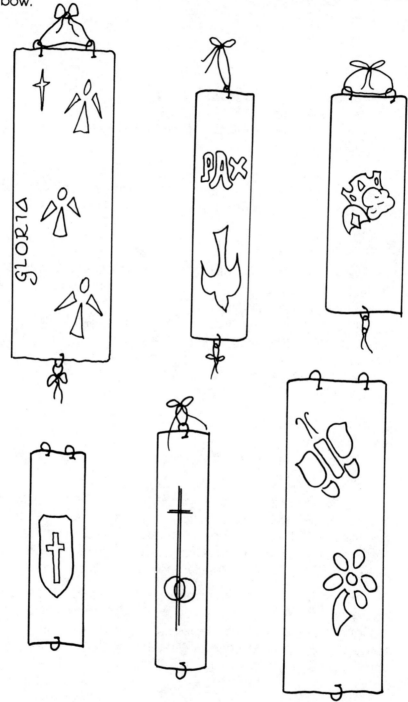

TREE OR HANGING ORNAMENTS

Most of the patterns in this book can be used to make simple flat ornaments: cut from felt (two pieces glued or stitched together), from styrofoam or balsa, or make from baker's clay.

Recipe for baker's clay:
    4 cups flour
    1 cup salt

Mix flour and salt together. Add slowly:
    $1\frac{1}{2}$ cups water
    1 tablespoon oil

Mix all ingredients for 4–5 minutes. Roll out and cut with cookie cutters or cardboard patterns and a sharp knife. Make a hole for string if ornament is to be hung. Bake at 350 degrees for one hour.

Stuffed ornaments can be made from two pieces of fabric, stitched together by hand or machine. Enlarge patterns, cut two pieces, sew together (wrong sides together), turn and stuff for pillows.

Angel

Shepherd

Three
Kings

MOBILES

The framework for any mobile may be a ring, two crossed dowels, a series of sticks or dowels of various lengths hung from one another, or a coat hanger. The secret is to achieve balance: feel free to experiment with the number of objects hung and the lengths of strings.

BAPTISMAL MOBILE

The symbols shown here are particularly appropriate for a gift at the time of baptism or christening, but are also suitable for a baby gift or birthday gift. In addition, since the early Christians were usually baptized or confirmed during the Easter Vigil the night of Holy Saturday, the mobile is a suitable Easter gift.

Materials:

One 10" metal or wood ring for framework and one cafe ring, about 1½" diameter.

Fabric: felt or assorted cotton or corduroy for emblems (colors may be bright or pastel; prints also work). Use white or very pale blue for cloud.

Fusible interfacing (one side only)—about ⅓ yard for cotton or corduroy fabrics. Felt does not require interfacing.

Stuffing: polyester fiberfill or old nylons. (Emblems may also be two pieces of felt, stitched together, unstuffed.)

Embroidery floss or liquid embroidery for details (optional). White satin ribbon: two yards ½" ribbon, 3½ yards ¼" ribbon, to cover ring and hang mobile.

Tracing paper, pencil, scissors, pins, sewing needle or machine and thread. Iron; craft glue.

Instructions:

Trace patterns and cut out. Fold fabric wrong sides together; place and pin patterns; cut out. Press fusible interfacing onto wrong sides of fabric (if you are using cotton or corduroy). Mark details with chalk, soap, or dressmaker's pencil; embroider or liquid embroider details.

Stitch emblems, right sides together, leaving about 2" open to turn; turn right side out, stuff, and hand catch remaining opening.

For rainbow and cloud: leave top of cloud open, leave underside of rainbow open. Turn right side out, stitch ends of rainbow into top seam of cloud by hand, stuff both, and finish stitching closed.

Wrap rings with 1/2" ribbon, using a spot of glue at beginning and end to hold in place. Wooden rings may be left natural or painted with enamel.

Cut 1/4" ribbon into five 24" lengths. Fold one end over cafe ring and glue or tack with white thread. The ribbons will overlap somewhat, but should not all be stacked in the same place.

Hang cafe ring from a cuphook or rod so that you have enough clear space to add the 10" ring and balance it. Mark four opposite points on 10" ring. Hold large ring the desired distance below the cafe ring (about 12" is good). Wrap four of the ribbons once or twice around the places you have marked. Glue or tack with thread, or pin in place until mobile is finished. The fifth ribbon should hang down through the center of the large ring.

Attach figures to ribbons as follows: measure desired length on the four outside ribbons, then pin to upper seam of stuffed emblem. Check to be sure mobile is balanced. If not, shorten or lengthen ribbon, or change the place it is pinned to emblem. When balance is correct, tack ribbon with thread to figures. Judge length of center ribbon by eye—the rainbow should hang slightly below the other figures. Attach rainbow to its ribbon.

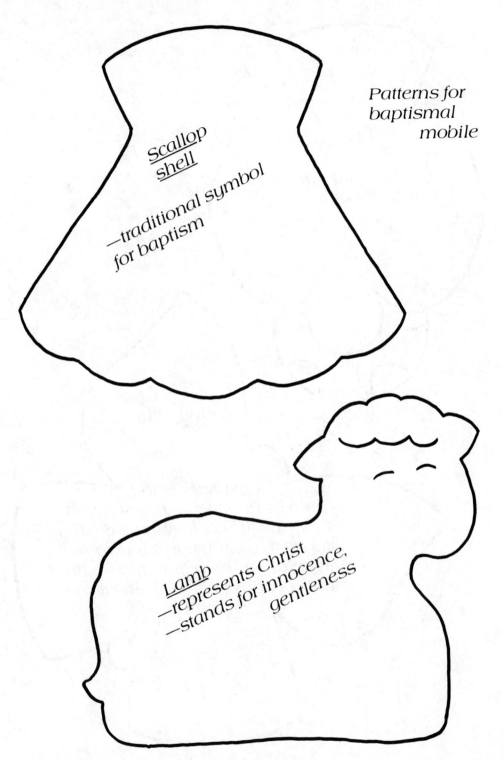

Patterns for
baptismal
mobile

Scallop
shell

—traditional symbol
for baptism

Lamb
—represents Christ
—stands for innocence,
gentleness

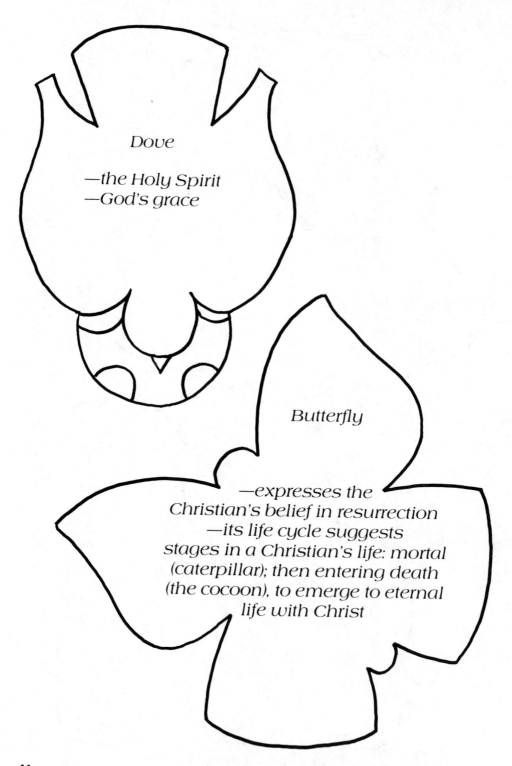

Dove

—the Holy Spirit
—God's grace

Butterfly

—expresses the
Christian's belief in resurrection
—its life cycle suggests
stages in a Christian's life: mortal
(caterpillar); then entering death
(the cocoon), to emerge to eternal
life with Christ

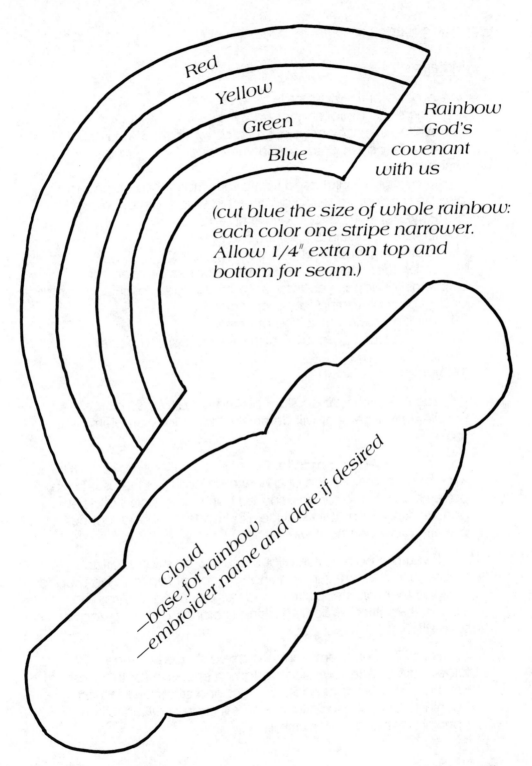

Red

Yellow

Green

Blue

Rainbow
—God's
covenant
with us

(cut blue the size of whole rainbow:
each color one stripe narrower.
Allow 1/4" extra on top and
bottom for seam.)

Cloud
—base for rainbow
—embroider name and date if desired

WEDDING MOBILE

Materials:

Two metal rings, 10" or 12" in diameter
One small metal ring for hanging
White satin ribbon: about 4 yards ½" wide, 3½ yards ¼"
wide; white cotton cord, carpet thread, or fishline to attach
emblems
Remnant or purchased fabric for emblems (emblems may
also be made from balsa or other thin wood, or from masonite)
Polyester stuffing for fabric emblems
Fusible interfacing, fusible bonding
(paint for balsa or other wood emblems)
Embroidery floss and needle or liquid embroidery for
emblems (optional: you may either embroider designs on shields
or cut from contrasting fabric and appliqué)
Thread, sewing machine or needle
Tracing paper, pencil, ballpoint pen, carbon paper

Instructions:

See illustration for possible alternative arrangements of
mobile—arrangement will determine how many emblems you
make.

For a twined-ring mobile, three, four, or five emblems will
work best. Decide which and how many you wish to use. Trace
patterns. Transfer to fabric using carbon paper and ballpoint
pen, working on a hard surface. (To transfer to wood, cut out
pattern, draw around it with pencil.)

If you are going to appliqué designs on shields, attach
fusible (one side only) interfacing to back of fabric to be used for
designs. Then transfer pattern and cut out. Bond designs to
shields, then stitch, if desired, using straight, narrow zig-zag, or
satin stitch.

For stuffed emblems, cut two shield shapes apiece from
folded fabric. After bonding design on one side (both if desired),
lay shield shapes right sides together and stitch, leaving an
opening about 1½" to 2" long for turning and stuffing. Stitch
opening by hand after stuffing.

Liquid or hand embroidery should also be done before shield shapes are stitched together.

For wood emblems, paint and make a small hole at top of shield for hanging line. Masonite should be sanded lightly or washed with deglosser or liquid sandpaper before painting. For wood such as plywood or pine, you may choose to use miniature screw eyes in top rather than drilling a hole for hanging.

To assemble mobile: Wind $\frac{1}{2}$" satin ribbon around rings, using a spot of glue at beginning and end. Overlap rings as shown, and fasten with white cord or thread. Attach thread or fishline to each emblem, using a needle, and knot near top of emblem; attach other end of line to ribbon on ring, again using needle and knotting. Attach $\frac{1}{4}$" satin ribbon to tops of two large rings and to top junction point; tack with needle and thread. Draw ends together through small ring, check for balance, and tack with needle and thread.

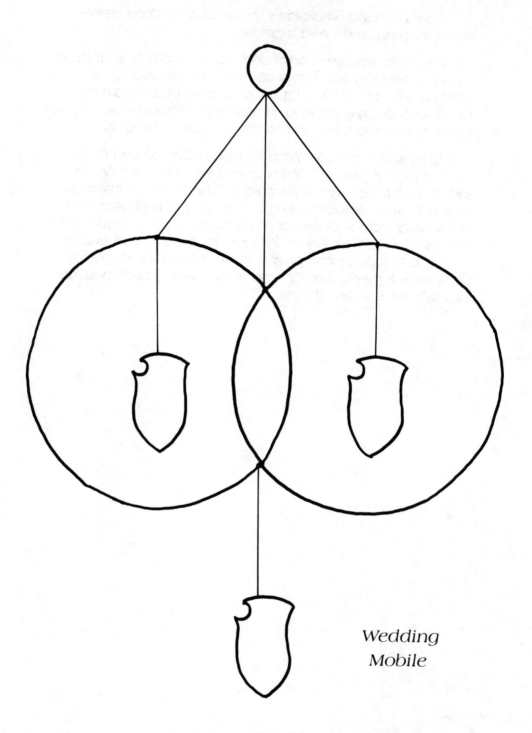

*Wedding
Mobile*

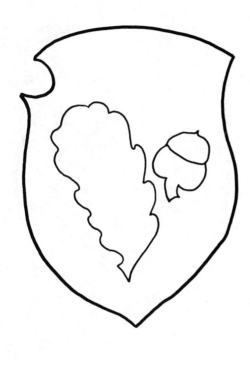

Emblems for
wedding mobile

—also suitable for door
or wall hangings
—enlarge to applique
on pillows or quilts

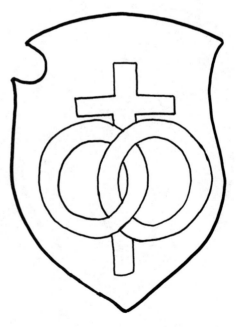

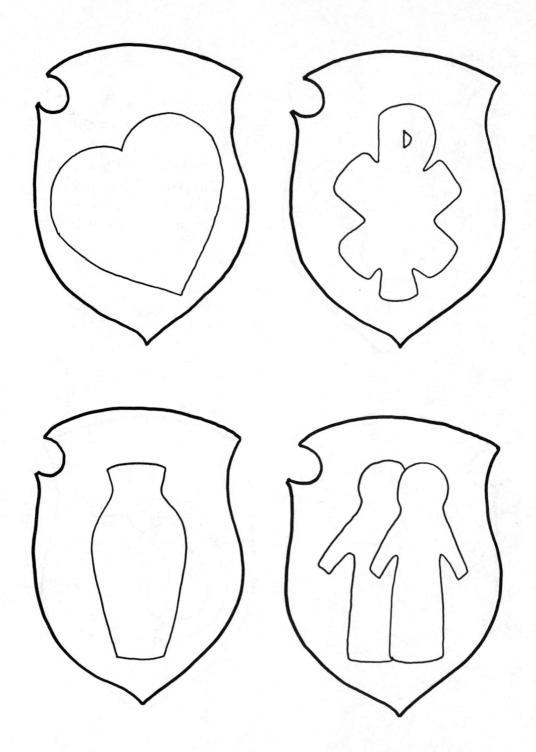

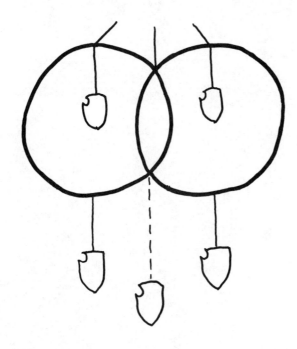

*Vertical rings with
four or five
emblems*

Mobile arrangements

16″ horizontal ring

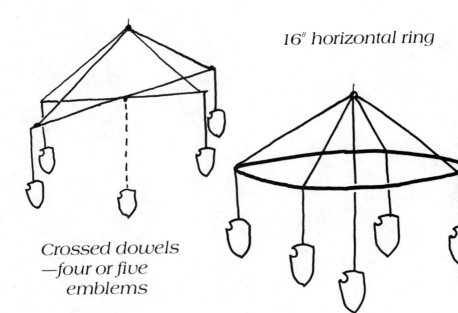

*Crossed dowels
—four or five
emblems*

V.   For the Household

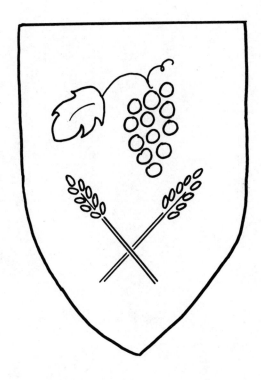

"Build houses, settle down;
plant gardens, and eat
what they produce."

Jeremiah 29:5

CUTTING BOARD, CHEESE BOARD, BREAD BOARD

Materials:

Pine, ash or walnut, about 1" thick and big enough for the size board you wish to make: may be as small as 6" × 8" or as large as 14" × 14", or 5" × 14" for a "French loaf" board.

Coping saw or jigsaw; sandpaper.

Paper, pencil, graph paper for enlarging or reducing designs if necessary.

Mineral oil for finishing.

Heavy glossy paper or magazine pictures for decoupage (optional: do not use on a board that is to be exposed to a great deal of moisture); instant decoupage.

Instructions:

Choose a pattern you would like to make. To make a shaped board, enlarge pattern, cut out, and trace onto wood with pencil. Cut out; sand thoroughly; rub in several coats of mineral oil.

For a plain board with a motif: cut out board and sand thoroughly; carve or woodburn design; rub with oil.

To decoupage: Cut out board and sand. Lay picture on board to check for placement, then remove. Put one coat of decoupage medium on board, lay picture down carefully, and smooth out bubbles. When dry, apply one to five more coats.

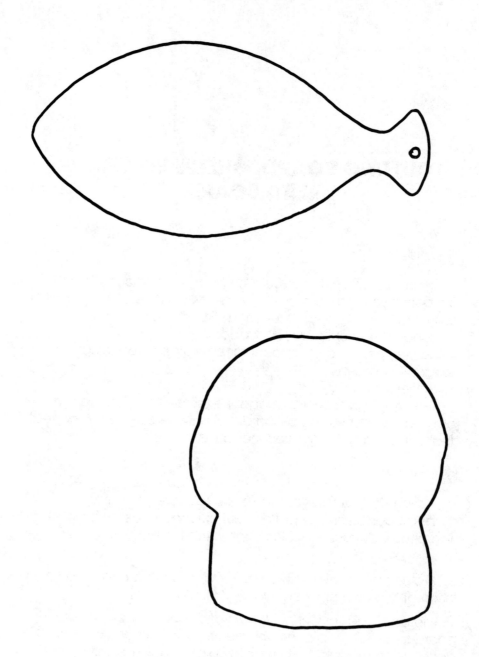

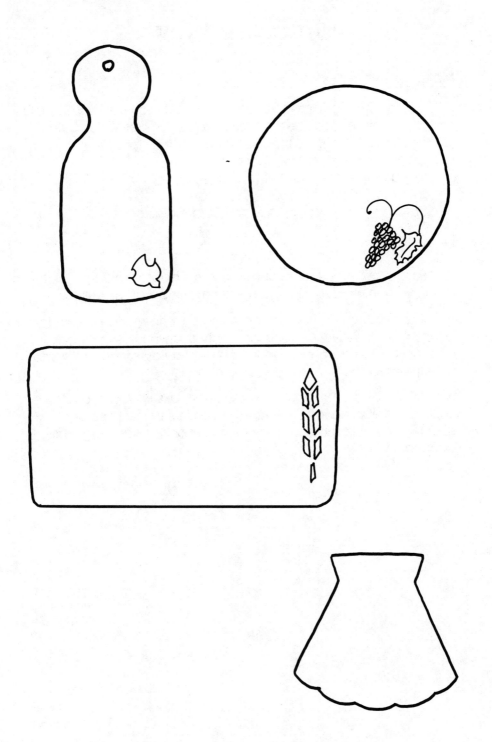

POTHOLDER RACK

Materials:

Wood—pine or plywood work well; you may also wish to use cherry or walnut for added beauty—some lumber stores carry scraps of these woods at moderate cost.
Coping saw or jigsaw; sandpaper
Hand drill or electric drill (optional)
2 - 4 cuphooks, at least $\frac{3}{4}$" diameter
Paint, varnish, decoupage medium if desired.

Instructions:

Follow general instructions for cutting boards, but finish with paint, varnish, or decoupage medium instead of mineral oil.

If desired, drill a hole at top or one in either end of rack for hanging. Alternatively, place one or two small nails in back of rack and add piano wire or waxed dental floss to hang. Or use pre-gummed picture hanging backings.

After wood is prepared, screw cuphooks into rack at desired places. It helps to work with real potholders to get a sense of spacing. If wood is hard, a screw-starter or drill can begin the cuphook holes.

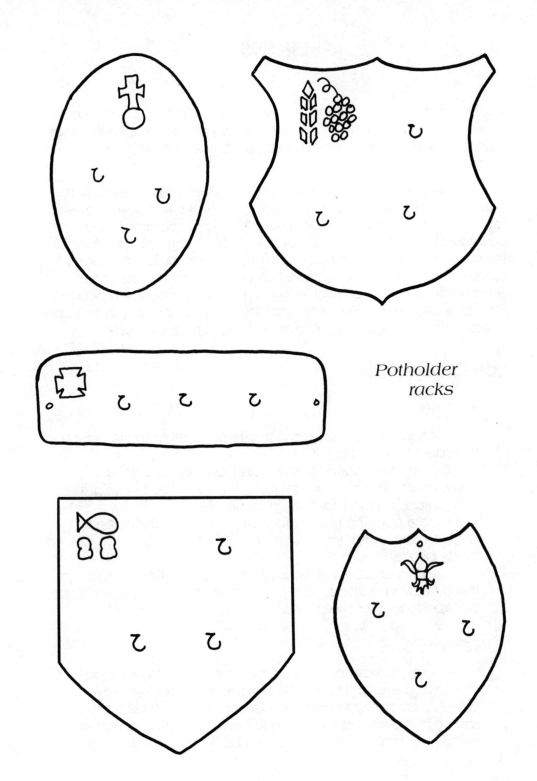

*Potholder
racks*

61

LINENS

Linens are particularly appropriate as wedding gifts, but may also be given at holiday times, as thank-you gifts for hospitality, or as going-away gifts to students or young people embarking on householding.

In addition to the items described, consider adding symbols or motifs to purchased spreads, blankets, sheets or pillowcases, towels, tablecloths, placemats, or potholders. To add an appliqué to a purchased item, choose a compatible fabric—one that will clean in the same way and will not shrink or fade. In most cases, the fabric for appliqués should be pre-washed before emblems are cut out. For extra body, or before embroidering on appliqué, back with bonded (one side only) interfacing. Add appliqué to purchased item by hand or machine stitching, using satin stitch around edges if desired.

ROUND TABLECLOTH

Materials:

60" square of cotton-polyester blend or other fabric you feel is suitable for a tablecloth.
Compatible fabric for emblems (you may choose a complementary color, or vary the fabric for different designs).
Thread, sewing machine, pins, needles
Fusible bonding (plus fusible one side only interfacing for backing emblems if you wish more body or wish to embroider on the appliqués)
Chalk or dressmaker's pencil; string; and a thumbtack or a friend (lacking a friend, you may wish to make the circle pattern on taped-together newspaper first, just in case)

Instructions:

Fold the square of cloth in half horizontally, then vertically, so you have a smaller square. Tie string to chalk or dressmaker's pencil, then stretch string from one corner to the folded point of square (the center of fabric). Thumbtack at center, or have a friend hold firmly. Make an arc with chalk from one outside point

Layout for ten-emblem tablecloth

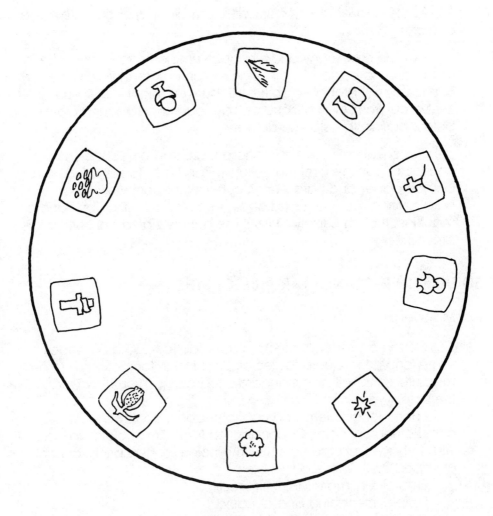

—symbols may be embroidered or appliqued onto background shapes or directly onto tablecloth.
—symbols in illustration represent events in the life of Christ.

to the other. Cut, and you have your circle. (If you feel insecure about doing this on the fabric, tape newspaper into a 60" square, fold, and follow the same procedure. Then you have a pattern to use on the fabric.)

Make a rolled hem or attach seam binding or braid to edge of cloth.

Decide how many and what size emblems you would like to place around edge of cloth. Eight or ten emblems cut from 6" or 8" squares will probably work best, but you might wish to do twelve cut from 4" or 6" squares. Lay squares out around cloth before cutting to help you decide.

Trace patterns you have chosen; enlarge or reduce as necessary (see general instructions). Transfer to fabric using carbon paper and hard pencil or ballpoint pen, working on a hard surface. Cut out, bond or pin to cloth, and stitch by hand or machine. If cloth is likely to fray, use narrow zig-zag or satin stitch around edges.

SQUARE OR RECTANGULAR TABLECLOTHS

Materials:

Cotton-polyester or other suitable fabric—52" to 54" wide; same length for square tablecloth, 68" to 70" for rectangle (these measurements will give standard-sized cloths—you may adapt the sizes if you wish).
Fabric for emblems: compatible fabric; contrasting or complementary color. Depending on formality of cloth, you may wish to have solid tablecloth with emblems in tiny prints, or print or striped cloth with solid emblems.
Embroidery materials, if desired
Fusible interfacing and bonding
Thread, needle, sewing machine

Instructions:

Pre-wash fabric and dry in dryer. Make rolled hems or turn under $\frac{1}{4}$", then turn again $\frac{1}{4}$" and stitch hem. Decide on size and number of emblems you wish to use. Follow instructions for round tablecloth to prepare emblems, being sure to lay out for placement and eye appeal before attaching.

Suggested types of emblems:

Flowers and plants of the Bible—these will be attractive embroidered on uniform backings. Do the embroidery before cutting shape out. Trace pattern, transfer to fabric with carbon, back fabric with fusible interfacing, place in embroidery hoop. You may do a series on a large piece of cloth, being sure to leave enough margin to cut shapes afterward.

Alternating loaves and fishes, or grapes and wheat. These may either be appliquéd outlines or embroidered on backings.

One or more crosses

Wedding symbols

Jesse Tree symbols

Christmas or Easter symbols

PLACEMATS

Materials:

Double-sided pre-quilted fabric: allow 13" or 14" by 18" for rectangular or oval mats; wedge shapes can be cut from same size. For round placemat, allow for 14" to 15" diameter. (See instructions for round tablecloth for procedure for cutting a circle.) Double-wide seam binding in contrasting or complementary color. Fabric for emblems, fusible interfacing.

Instructions:

Cut out placemats. Cut out emblems and back with fusible interfacing. Lay emblem on placemat, check for placement, pin in place. Then sandwich edge nearest emblem into binding to see if emblem still looks well placed; adjust if necessary, and repin. Remove binding; bond or stitch emblem down. Repeat for all mats. Finally, place seam binding around placemat, encasing edges and folding under at end. Pin or baste, and stitch through all thicknesses.

NAPKINS

Materials:

Polyester-cotton blend in a color that matches, contrasts with, or complements tablecloth or placemats.

Fabric for emblems or embroidery materials, if you wish. Fusible interfacing.

Thread and needle or sewing machine. Amount to allow: for luncheon napkins, allow 14" to 16"; for dinner napkins, allow 18" to 21".

Instructions:

Cut number and size of napkins you want. (Ideally, fabric should be pre-washed and dried.) Make rolled hems or fold under $\frac{1}{4}$" all around, then $\frac{1}{4}$" again, and stitch down.

For emblems, you will probably want only one per napkin, placed in a corner. You may wish to reduce it in size or use the same size you have placed on tablecloth or placemats. You may also wish to embroider directly on napkins.

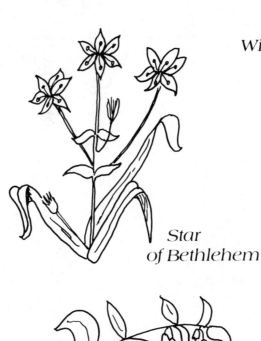

Star
of Bethlehem

Wildflowers with
* Biblical names*
* —check field guides*
*   for more*
* —use for embroidery*
*   patterns*

Solomon's
Seal

Jacob's
Ladder

Golden
Jerusalem
(Black-eyed
Susan)

Aaron's
Rod

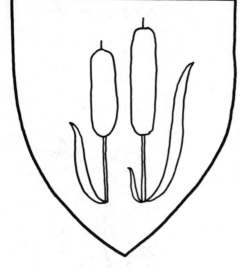

Bulrush
—hope of salvation

Red Carnation
—pure love

Oak
—faith and endurance

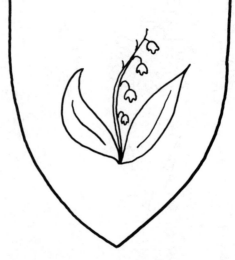

Lily of the Valley
—humility

VI.   For Wearing

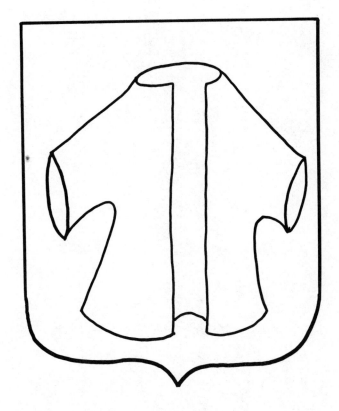

*"Then they made the tunics
of finely woven linen..."*

Exodus 39:27

SHIRTS OF ALL SORTS

Appliqué, fabric crayons, or embroidery (hand, liquid, and machine, depending on your tastes and talents) can personalize homemade or purchased shirts for almost any occasion. A few general hints: buttonfront shirts are probably most easily decorated on the back or on the front pocket. If using liquid embroidery be sure to have layers of newspaper underneath—and between the pocket and the body of the shirt. Men's white short-sleeved undershirts are inexpensive and make wonderful nightshirts: use small for young children, extra-large for teenagers and small adults. The secret of the nightshirt is that it should be baggy.

Purchased T-shirts in light colors, sweatshirts, and some jackets can all be decorated using the media listed.

CHILDREN'S NIGHTSHIRT (adults might like it too)

Materials: A too-large men's undershirt
        lightweight solid-color knit fabric (an old undershirt will do) OR lightweight polyester/cotton fabric
    Fusible (one side) interfacing for back of appliqué
    (Optional: a second piece of fabric in a different color—for foot of bed)
    Fusible bonding
    Tracing paper and pencil; embroidery floss and needle OR liquid embroidery for the prayer.

Instructions:

Trace the pattern, including lettering. Lay on fabric and cut out. If you are using a different color for foot of bed, lay pattern on that fabric and cut using inner line plus ¼" (woven fabric only) to turn under hem.

Bond interfacing to back of appliqué, and trim away excess.

Bond foot of bed to bed (if using woven fabric, first press under ¼").

Lettering:

Place appliqué on hard surface. Lay pattern over appliqué with carbon paper between. Draw over lettering with hard pencil or ballpoint pen. Remove pattern and carbon. Embroider or liquid embroider.

Place finished appliqué on front of shirt and pin in place. Hand or machine stitch to shirt. (If possible, do satin stitch in hand or machine embroidery around outline and foot of bed; otherwise, use small zigzag stitch or two to three rows of straight stitching.)

NOTE: appliqué can be used on fabric to make a bedtime-prayer wall hanging. Pattern can be enlarged for bedspreads or crib quilts.

T-SHIRTS AND SWEATSHIRTS

Materials:

Any purchased or homemade T-shirt or sweatshirt.

Fabric for appliqués (see nightshirt instructions; felt also works IF the garment is washed in cold water or lukewarm water and not dried in the dryer; some fabric stores and craft departments now carry wool-synthetic blended felts which require less care).

Embroidery floss and needles or machine; or liquid embroidery or fabric crayon. Fusible interfacing and bonding.

Tracing paper, pencil; graph paper and ruler, plain paper if you wish to reduce or enlarge pattern.

Instructions:

Choose an emblem or motif you like. Trace, then reduce or enlarge if you wish. Transfer to shirt using carbon paper and a hard pencil or ballpoint pen, or cut out emblem and use as pattern. Transfer is preferable if you wish to keep the pattern intact but need to cut several pieces.

Embroider or liquid embroider design on shirt, being sure to use paper between layers of shirt, between shirt and pocket, or under a shirt back.

If you prefer to appliqué, transfer design to appliqué fabric. Follow instructions for appliqué in nightshirt pattern.

NOTE: As with the bedtime prayer, many shirt designs are suitable for spreads, hangings, even pillow covers or cases.

Bond interfacing to back of appliqué, and trim away excess. Bond foot of bed to bed (if using woven fabric, first press under ¼").

Lettering: place appliqué on hard surface. Lay pattern over appliqué with carbon paper between. Draw over lettering with hard pencil or ballpoint pen. Remove pattern and carbon. Embroider or liquid embroider.

Place finished appliqué in front of shirt and pin in place. Hand or machine stitch to shirt. (If possible, do satin stitch in hand or machine embroidery around outline and foot of bed; otherwise, use small zigzag stitch or two to three rows of straight stitching.)

NOTE: appliqué can be used on fabric to make a bedtime-prayer wall hanging. Pattern can be enlarged for bedspreads or crib quilts.

"Let my prayer be set forth in your sight as incense, the lifting up of my hands as the evening sacrifice." (Psalm 141:2)

All-purpose emblems

Namesake shirts—symbols for apostles and saints

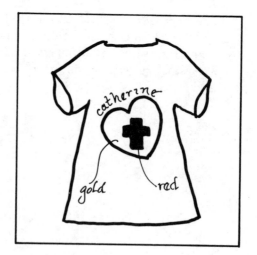

Matthew
Mark
Luke and John
Guard the bed
that I lie on

Keep watch, dear Lord,
with those who work
or watch
or weep
this night
and give your angels charge
over those who sleep

"DESIGNER LABELS"

You can label any clothing you sew for someone else or purchased clothing. After all: the Lord God Jehovah is also a famous designer!

Materials:

1" to 1½" wide grosgrain or satin ribbon; about 1½" long or longer

Pencil or dressmaker's pencil to draw motif

Embroidery needle and floss

Instructions:

There are two basic styles of label, folded and unfolded. For a folded label, fold ribbon, matching cut ends, press crease. Draw design, centering it in the area ⅜" from crease. Embroider through both thicknesses, using running stitch, back-stitch, or satin stitch. Begin and end stitching inside the folded ribbon.

For an unfolded label, you may wish to attach fusible (one side only) interfacing to back for extra body. Fold cut ends under ⅛" to ¼". Embroider design or lettering horizontally on ribbon.

To attach labels: Place patch pocket on homemade garment; for purchased garment, loosen stitching of pocket carefully with seam ripper. Lift edge of pocket and place open edges of label underneath, allowing about ½" seam. Top stitch pocket and label by machine or hand.

Lay unfolded label near top or side edge of shirt pocket or hip pocket. Attach with bar tacks at either end, or hand-catch to pocket.

To attach into a seam: for a purchased garment, cut seam threads carefully with a seam ripper. Place cut edges of label into seam, pin in place. With garment wrong side out, restitch the seam by hand or machine, catching in the label. For a homemade garment, lay one side of garment right side up and place cut edges of label toward cut edge of seam (probably label edges will not come all the way to seam edge—check to be sure enough label will stick out of garment when you have finished). Lay other garment piece, right side down, over first. Pin carefully through both garment pieces and label. Stitch seam as you normally would.

Several designs and placements are illustrated—but let your imagination be your guide.

"Designer Labels"

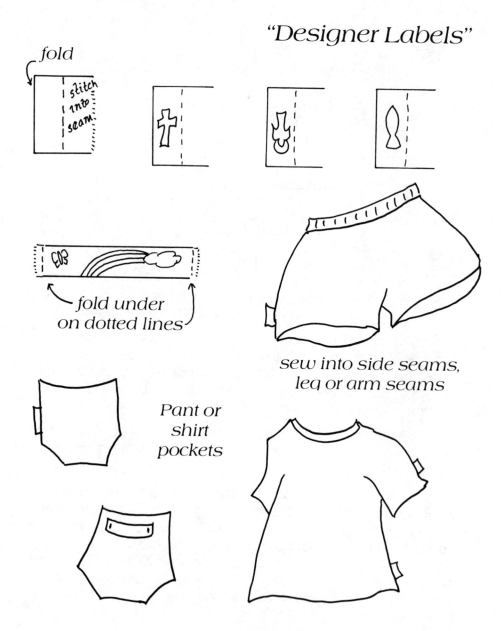

fold

stitch into seam

fold under on dotted lines

sew into side seams, leg or arm seams

Pant or shirt pockets

ROBES AND CAFTANS

"His tunic was without seam,
woven from top to bottom."
(John 19:23)

SEAMLESS ROBE

A seamless robe such as Jesus wore would have been woven on a wide loom. To create a similar robe, take a 60" wide piece of fabric (velour, lightweight corduroy and washable wool are good fabrics for winter robes; use cottons and blends for summer). The fabric should be twice the desired length—from shoulder to floor for a full-length robe, shoulder to knee for tunic length. Add up to 6" to the length to allow for a hem.

Directions:

Fold fabric in half crosswise and cut desired shape.
Cut a slit 8" long in the center of the fold—from the center point to 4" on either side.

Finish raw edges along sides and underarms with binding or a narrow hem. You may wish to add purchased fringe—if so, leave it unstitched toward the bottom of the robe until hem is finished.

Turn up bottom and stitch hem. Bottom may be trimmed with braid. Stitch fringe the rest of the way, if necessary.

Provide a sash of the same fabric or a cotton "rope" sash can be purchased in the notions section of department and fabric stores. The sash should be about 6' long.

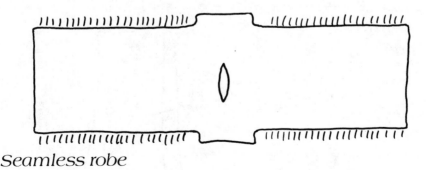

Seamless robe

Finally, trim neck opening with seam binding or braid, or turn under a narrow hem.

You may choose to seam the garment at the sides. If so, turn right sides together and sew a continuous seam from bottom to sleeve edge, curving at underarm and clipping curve. Finish neck and hem as above.

A fringe trim may be added to a seamed robe: lay the robe open, right side of fabric up. Place fringe down one side, from about 2″ below underarm curve to 3″ above bottom edge. Finished edge of fringe should match edge of fabric, and the fringe itself should be pointing toward the center of garment. Pin or baste in place. Repeat with opposite side. Then fold robe crosswise, right sides together, and stitch seam.

Variations may include "angel sleeves," gathered sleeves, a slit in one or both sides, a wider bottom, or a sleeveless robe (see illustrations).

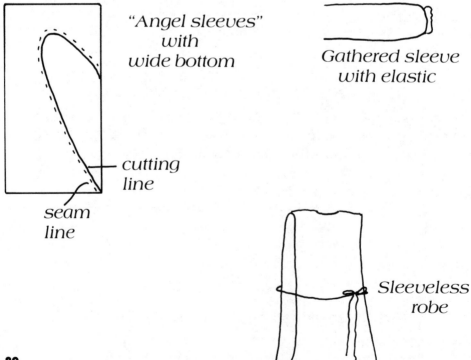

"Angel sleeves" with wide bottom

Gathered sleeve with elastic

cutting line

seam line

Sleeveless robe

THREE-PIECE ROBES

Some biblical robes would have been woven on narrower looms and would consist of three pieces—two for the skirts and one incorporating bodice and sleeves. Such a robe can be made very simply from two or three bath towels. Three towels will make a long robe; if you use two, cut one in half crosswise for the two skirts, which will be about knee length. The exact size of the garment will be determined by the size of the towels, and children's robes can be made from smaller towels. Remember that the ancient Israelites did not have commercial patterns, so all sizes were approximate. Even length was changed by means of looping a garment up over the sash if it needed to be shortened.

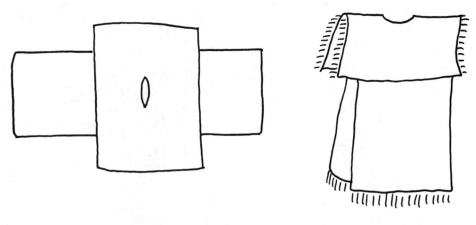

Three-piece robe   *Robe made of towels*

JOSEPH'S "COAT OF MANY COLORS"

Joseph's "coat of many colors" may have been a "coat of many pieces." Although we cannot know for sure, we may give "Joseph's coats" of different types to those we love. One type, of course, is of purchased multi-colored fabric. The colors most frequently mentioned in the Bible are blue, scarlet, and purple, but we don't need to be limited to them.

Another type of Joseph's coat might be made of fabric remnants, stitched into long strips and joined together, then fashioned into a robe.

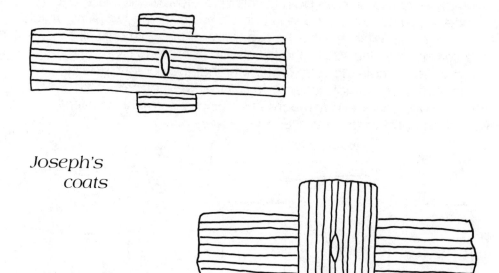

Joseph's
coats

To make long strips of fabric, cut material at a 45 degree angle and stitch together. It's a good idea to open the two pieces before stitching, to be sure you have a straight strip—I sometimes do it backward!

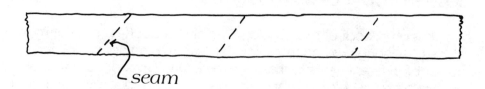

seam

Strip for Joseph's coat

VII.   For Children

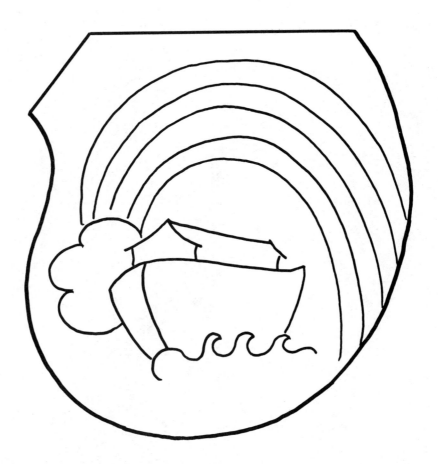

"And the squares of the city
will be full
of boys and girls
playing in the squares."

Zechariah 8:5

PLAYTHINGS

Long before toy companies, children amused themselves with sticks and stones, scraps of animal skins, and pieces of bone. Pitching objects at targets, throwing and juggling balls, dice, board games such as chess, and toys such as dolls or miniature replicas of adult boats or chariots were all part of daily life in the ancient world.

SKITTLES

Materials:

A piece of scrap lumber—pine or plywood, about $\frac{3}{4}$" to 1" thick, and about 5" by 9"
Three round clothespins
Three marbles or round stones
Saw and craft saw or coping saw; sandpaper
Paint or varnish (optional)

Instructions:

Mark three arches in wood (see illustration), and cut out. Sand wood thoroughly; paint or stain if desired.

Cut clothespins about 2" down from top; sand bottom edges; paint or stain if desired.

Give the wall, the figures and the marbles (perhaps in a small cloth pouch), with the directions that the object of the game is to set the figures somewhat behind the arch and knock them down by rolling the marbles. Any number can play, but only one can go at a time.

WOODEN BALL

Materials:

A block of wood 3" to 4" in diameter
Sharp carving knife
Rasp; sandpaper
Paint, stain, varnish, wax if desired

Instructions:

Carve corners off the wood block, and rough out a ball shape. Finish by using rasp until ball feels right, then sand.

Wood may be left natural, rubbed with mineral oil or wax, painted, or stained and varnished.

FABRIC OR LEATHER BALL

Materials:

Small cork
Strips of scrap cloth or leather, about $\frac{1}{2}$" to 1" wide, of varying lengths; unbleached muslin for outer layer
Craft glue
Acrylic paints or permanent felt-tip markers (optional)

Instructions:

Starting with small strips of cloth, wind tightly around cork, gluing starting and finishing ends and alternating direction. Continue until you have the size and shape you want. The ball will not be perfectly round. Make the topmost layer of unbleached muslin strips, and paint or add designs.

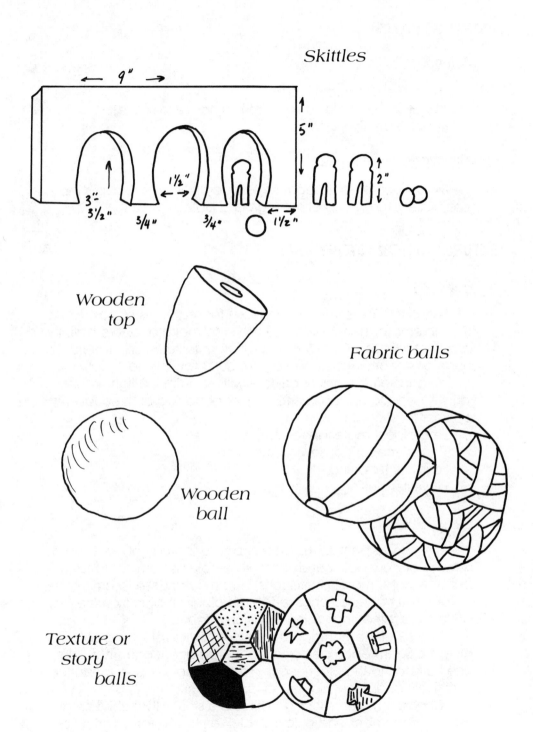

Skittles

9"

5"

3"
3½"
3/4"
3/4"
1½"
1½"
2"

Wooden
top

Fabric balls

Wooden
ball

Texture or
story
balls

JUGGLING BALLS

Materials:

Three old dead tennis balls
About ¾ cup of lead shot (from a hardware store)
Epoxy glue; fabric tape

Instructions:

Slit an inch or so in seam of each ball, fill with ¼ cup shot, glue closed, run a strip of tape around ball.

TEXTURE BALL OR "STORY BALL"

Materials:

Scrap fabric—some large pieces for segments of ball; fabric for emblems for story ball. If you prefer to make a texture ball, try to collect fabrics with at least six different textures. Silk, taffeta, suede or smooth leather, velveteen, corduroy, crepe, wool, denim, and soft cottons or chiffons will do. With the lighter fabrics you will need to use an interfacing, or bond two or three layers together for strength.
Embroidery materials for story ball
Thread, needle or sewing machine
Fusible interfacing
Polyester stuffing

Instructions:

Cut twelve pentagons for one ball, using any of the sizes shown. For story ball, cut six or more emblems from scrap fabric, bond to six (or more) pentagons. (You may choose to embroider details. You may also choose to embroider emblems on the pentagons rather than using additional fabric.)

Sew six of the pentagons together as illustrated; repeat with other six. Seam each pentagon to the adjacent one. Then join one half-ball to the other, leaving the last edge open for stuffing. Stuff firmly and stitch shut by hand.

Choose emblems that go with Bible stories that children are likely to remember and enjoy; or pick emblems for a variety of saints.

Pentagon for stuffed ball—cut twelve

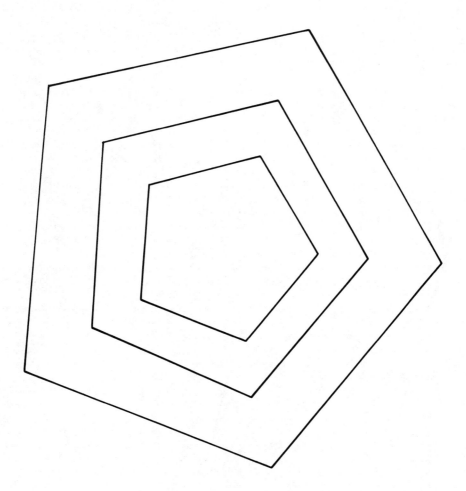

Make a set, one of each size, if you wish.

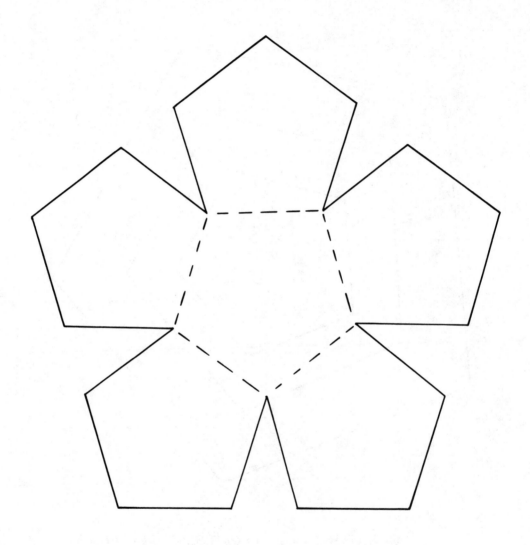

Layout for half of stuffed ball

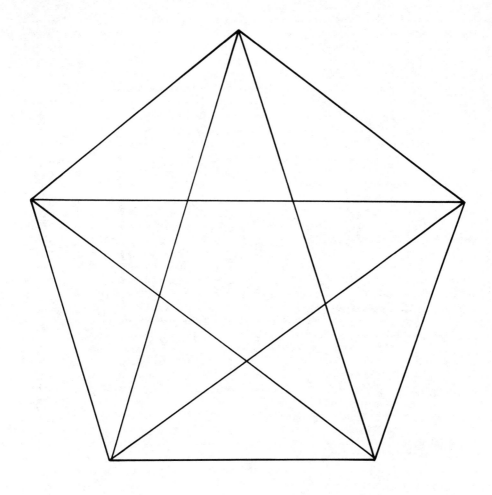

Pentagon may be used to make a
star pattern.

(for smaller stars, see other pentagon
   patterns: trace and join points
   as illustrated above.)

Cloth blocks
(3″ to 6″ squares)

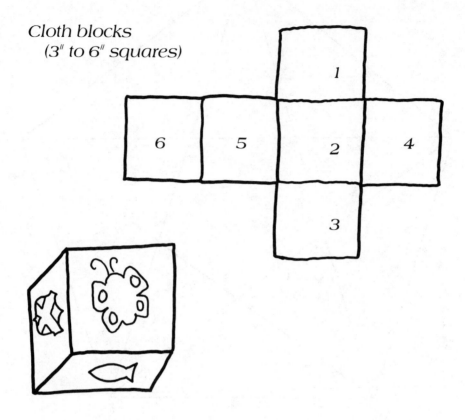

—embroider or applique six squares
—allow 1/4″ seams
—stitch together as shown,—then
      stitch 1 and 3 to 4 and 5
      (wrong sides together). Stitch 6—
      leaving opening to turn
—turn right side out; stuff;
      stitch closed by hand.
         (see directions for
           stuffed ball.)

TENTS

CARD TABLE TENT

Any tent is a magical place for a child, and the simplest is a sheet or blanket draped across two straight-backed chairs or hung over a clothesline in the yard. But I sometimes wonder, when I see the Christmas catalogues with elaborate fiberboard playhouses and "log cabins," if anyone makes card table tents any more. My sister and I as children were given a circus tent, made of pink-striped fabric, with animals appliquéd around the bottom and a jaunty red pennant at the peak. Our imaginations, of course, allowed it to be many things. Depending on the appliqués you choose, you can give a tent for Israelites wandering in the desert, or a tent that is Noah's Ark itself.

Materials:

(Finished size will be about 37" high, 34" square, for a 28" high 34" square card table):

Felt (3$\frac{1}{4}$ yd., 72" wide); or denim, heavy cotton, other sturdy fabric—6$\frac{1}{2}$ yd., 36" fabric.

Assorted scraps or remnants for appliqués.

Pencil, ruler, yardstick, paper for pattern, scissors; pinking shears (optional—for use with felt or non-woven fabric tent and appliqués); pins, thread, sewing machine, iron, craft glue, fusible bonding (optional).

One $\frac{3}{8}$" metal grommet and grommet setter (usually packaged with grommets, used with a hammer).

Plywood: 8" square of $\frac{1}{4}$" or $\frac{1}{2}$" plywood (or any scrap lumber such as pine)

Dowels: One 1" diameter, 15" long; one $\frac{1}{4}$" diameter, $9\frac{1}{2}$" long for flag or pennant.

Drill with a $\frac{1}{4}$" bit

Instructions:

Measure width and height of table. Add 1" to width, $\frac{1}{2}$" to height, *plus* an extra 1" to width if you are using 36" fabric which will need to be seamed to make side panels. If using woven fabric which will need to be hemmed at bottom, allow another $\frac{1}{4}$" to $\frac{1}{2}$" of height. Cut three panels this size from felt. Divide width measurement by two and cut 6 panels (be sure to add the extra for seam) from narrower fabric.

For front of tent: cut two pieces the same height as side panels, but each 12" narrower than a full side panel.

Seam side panels, if using woven fabric, and hem lower edges. Hem the cut edges of front center flaps. Overlap front center flaps so that the front panel measures the same size as side panels, and baste in place.

TOP:

Make a paper pattern by drawing a line the width of the table plus 1", and mark the center point. Mark a point 22" above center of line, and connect with ends of line to form a triangle. Draw a line parallel to base, $\frac{3}{4}$" below tip of triangle, and cut off tip. Cut four pieces of fabric using this pattern.

NOTE: if you are using narrower woven fabric, fold triangle pattern in half and cut from doubled fabric, allowing $\frac{1}{2}$" extra for seam. Seam triangular panels if necessary.

Appliqués:

Cut 16 appliqués from contrasting fabric. (For Noah's Ark, cut 8 pairs of animals.) If appliqués are approximately 4" × 4", place them two inches from bottom edge, about 3" from corner, and 4" apart. Lay out and check for spacing, then glue or bond to side panels. (You may choose to stitch around edges with zigzag or embroidery stitching, especially if using woven fabric for appliqués).

Assembling tent:

Attach base of one triangle to top of one panel, using ½″ seam; repeat for other panels. If you are using felt, you may place wrong sides together and allow seams to show on outside; otherwise, place right sides together for finished seam.

Join two sections with ½″ seam, sewing from bottom to top; add third section, then fourth section. You may wish to save front section for last, as it is somewhat bulkier.

Make two patches about 4″ square. If felt, you may pink edges; if woven, hem edges. Or use iron-on patches. Turn tent inside out and center one patch over opening at peak; pin or baste and stitch. Attach second square on outside. Cut small hole in center and attach grommet.

BASE: Center 1″ dowel over plywood base, and drive nail through plywood into dowel. For flag: drill 1″ deep hole in top of dowel. Place base in center of card table, fit tent over dowel and table, centering the peak over the dowel. Make flag by rolling edge of fabric or stiff paper around ¼″ dowel; insert bottom of flagpole through grommet into hole in 1″ dowel.

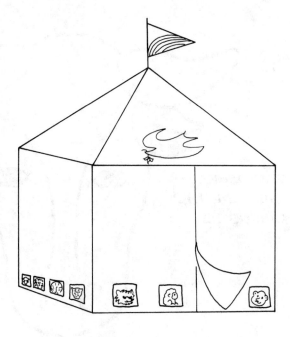

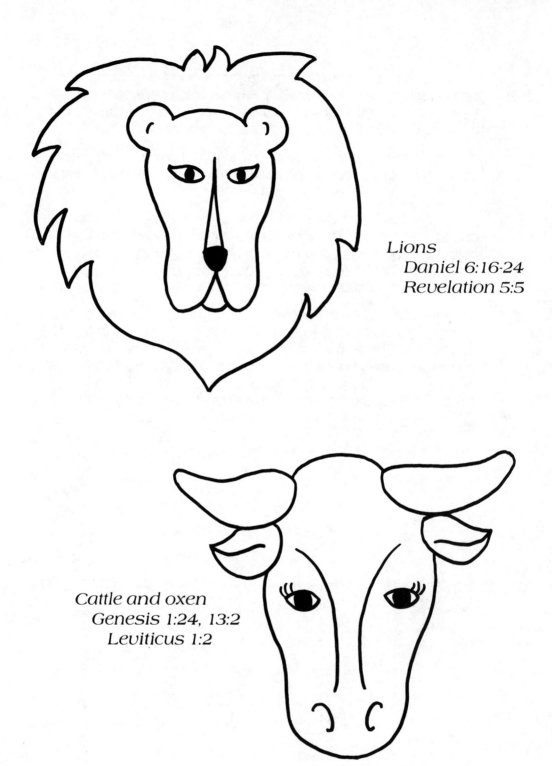

Lions
Daniel 6:16-24
Revelation 5:5

Cattle and oxen
Genesis 1:24, 13:2
Leviticus 1:2

Goats
    Genesis 27:9
    Exodus 26:7
    Matthew 25:32

Apes and monkeys
    I Kings 9:22

Foxes
Judges 15:4

Bears
I Samuel 17:34-36
II Samuel 17:8
II Kings 2:24

Peacocks
  I Kings 9:22

Leopards
  Isaiah 11:6
  Jeremiah 13:23

Two dove patterns
(Genesis 8:8-12)

—dove may be placed on
flag or roof

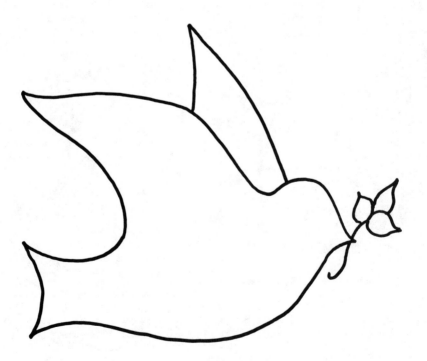

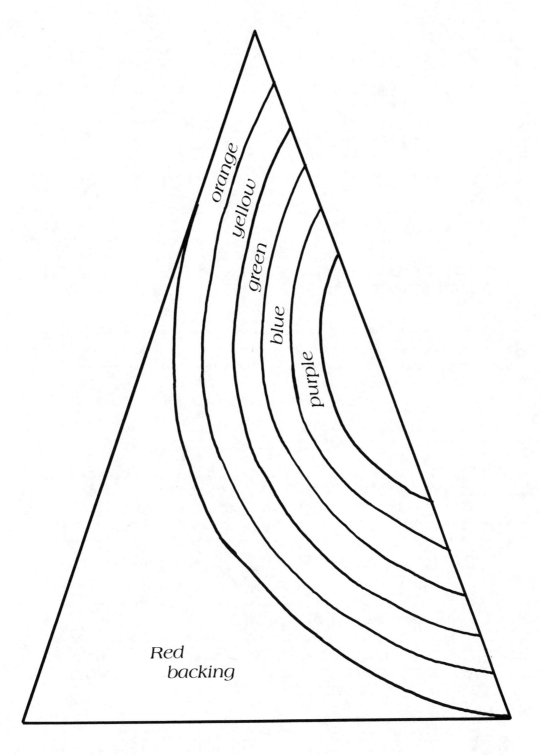

orange

yellow

green

blue

purple

Red
backing

"NOMAD TENT"

Materials:

An old blanket or sheet, or a piece of fabric of approximately the same size.

Fabric remnants for appliqués; fusible interfacing and bonding; embroidery materials (optional)

A length of clothesline or heavy twine about 4' longer than the blanket is wide; four lengths of stout cord, about 18" each (optional)

Instructions:

Select emblems you wish to put on tent and trace. Bond fabric for appliqués to fusible (one side only) interfacing, and cut out designs. Hand, machine, or liquid embroider details if desired.

Lay out emblems along bottom edges of tent; check for eye-appeal. Start about 10" from corners. If emblems are approximately 8", four per side should be enough. If they are 4" to 6", you may easily use five per side, perhaps six. A larger emblem or two may be added farther up on side of tent.

Pin or bond emblems to tent, then finish with hand or machine stitching—satin stitch or narrow zig-zag.

How to use the tent: Outdoors, string clothesline between two trees or posts, throw tent over line; tie one length of cord around each bunched corner, pull away from center to spread tent open, and hold with a rock or tie to a stick or tent peg. Indoors, you may also choose to throw the tent over clothesline (in the basement, for example; or tied to two pieces of furniture).

However, the tent may equally well be thrown over a chair back or two chairs near each other. Although the tent is not intended for "real camping," it provides endless hours of amusement indoors or out, and can serve as a familiar place to sleep if you are staying with friends or in motels while traveling with children. And if you have made it from a blanket, you can always *use* it as a blanket!

The emblems you choose may all have to do with a particular story—such as the story of Noah's Ark—or may represent a variety of characters and events—such as the Jesse Tree symbols. Tell a story relating to one or more of the emblems, say a prayer, and you have established a comforting sleep-time ritual at home or away.

Nomad Tent

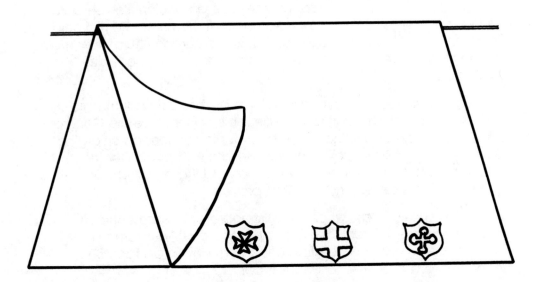

DOLLS AND PUPPETS

The representation of the human shape is probably one of the oldest forms of toy. Carved dolls have been found in Egyptian graves and in early Christian catacombs. Simple clay figures with depressions in the chest may have been given, with a Christening coin in the depression, by a child's godparents in the middle ages. And crèches, with figures of the Holy Family, the Magi, and the shepherds, found a place in both homes and churches in the middle ages, much as they do today.

A doll or puppet, or a set, appropriately costumed and given with a Bible (bookmarked at the relevant story), or a handwritten script or story makes a complete gift or can be a "starter" to be added to on future holidays. (These make nice gifts both for children and for parents and teachers.)

A "found" doll might represent the type an ancient Jewish child would play with, since the Jews did not craft the human form. Look for sticks or driftwood in shapes similar to the human figure; they may be painted or dressed in scraps of cloth made into robes (see illustration).

Any handmade or purchased doll may also be costumed to represent Biblical characters: enlarge robe pattern (see the General Directions at the beginning of this book for instructions on enlarging). Give a young child a stick or clothespin doll with a robe for the child to put on and take off, and let the child hold the doll and talk to it as you share Bible stories and bedtime prayers.

Dollhouses of clay, wood, or cardboard can represent dwellings of Bible times. Small tents, such as the people of Abraham's time might have lived in, can be fashioned from any scrap fabric, attached to a cork or wood base if desired.

Hand puppets are easily made from paper bags, socks, and fabric. "Human puppets" from paper grocery bags with the kids themselves inside are also great fun (see the instructions which follow).

Clothespin doll

Basic robe pattern
—trace for clothespin dolls
—cut two. Seam at shoulders,
under arm and sides. Cut
along dotted line for open
front. Unslit robe with
deeper rounded or squared
neck in front makes woman's dress.
—Enlarge for other dolls.
—Use scraps of fabric for turbans,
belts and shawls.

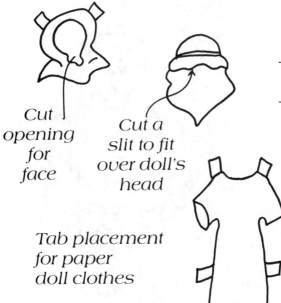

Cut
opening
for
face

Cut a
slit to fit
over doll's
head

To make paper dolls:
—trace figures from
coloring books
—cut from shirtboard or
other light cardboard,
or from styrofoam such
as vegetable trays

Tab placement
for paper
doll clothes

Replica of Egyptian doll
   —carve or cut with
      coping saw from 1/2"
      pine or plywood

   —glue on hair of yarn,
twine, or macrame cord
   —paint clothing or
geometric shapes on body

Driftwood doll
   —"found" shape

Cloth
   doll
      in
         robe

Greek "dancing doll"
   —make from clay or carved
wood; wire for joints.

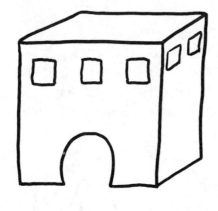

Simple dollhouse: make
from cardboard box or
baker's clay.
—roof may be removable
(Mark 2:1-12)
—house may have
two levels
—put "grass" on roof

Nomad tent and card table tent
may also be made small to accommodate
doll families or tribes.

Put card table
tent over cardboard
or wooden box, or
over a parson's table

"Abraham Tent." Make from
scrap leather, denim, or
other fabric. Fasten to
wooden base with nails, or
use outdoors, securing
with wooden pegs.
Shape may
be irregular.

Mitten puppet
  —trace around hand
  —sew two pieces together
  —sew or glue fabric for
    face and clothing, or draw
    with marker

Tunic for
mitten puppet

Paper bag
puppets

—stuff head
  with
  newspaper
—cardboard
  tube for neck
—tie string
  tightly around
  neck
—cut arm
  openings

Insert index finger
into neck tube, thumb and
second finger through
arm openings.

Rest tips of
fingers at edge of
fold. Move flap
up and down.
  Put either eyes
or mouth on
flap.

Costumes or "living puppets"
—Any size bag...

Cover body

...or head

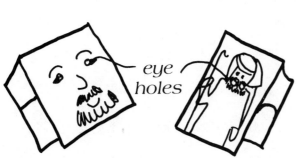

eye holes

Draw face only... or whole character

—for big people, cut out most or all of side panel, rather than just armholes

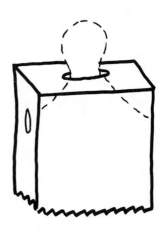

Cut hole for head, let bag rest on shoulders

109

MUSICAL INSTRUMENTS

"Praise the Lord! . . . Praise him with trumpet sound; praise him with lute and harp! Praise him with timbrel and dance; praise him with strings and pipe! Praise him with sounding cymbals; praise him with loud clashing cymbals!"

(Psalm 150:1, 3–5)

Trumpets

A trumpet is a tube with a small enough mouthpiece so that the mouth can seal it. The trumpeter changes tone by changing mouth tension and blowing force. Trumpets in biblical times were animal horns and conch shells. You can still find animal horns at flea markets and country sales, and can turn them into trumpets with the addition of a trumpet or cornet mouthpiece.

HOSE TRUMPET:

Materials:

A length of plastic or rubber tubing, at least two feet long
Plastic funnel
Trumpet or cornet mouthpiece (optional)

Instructions:

Place funnel in one end of tube, mouthpiece in the other.

A mouthpiece is suitable for an older child, 9 or 10 years; smaller children will blow, hum, or sing through a plain end happily.

DERDERS:

Any child, given a cardboard roll, will blow and sing into it until it disintegrates. Adults who believe they can't sing will also make music with derders. A complete set of derders—a derder choir, if you will—can be fashioned from a toilet paper roll (soprano derder); a paper towel roll (alto); a long skinny Christmas paper wrapping roll (tenor); and a fat wrapping paper roll or a rug or fabric tube (bass).

Materials:

    One or more cardboard rolls
    Contact paper, shelf paper, or fabric to cover
    Felt markers
    Glue

Instructions:

Cut paper as wide as tube is long. Roll tube in paper so that it is covered with about ½" left over. Run a line of glue lengthwise along tube, place one edge of paper on glue and allow to dry. Roll tube tightly in paper, and seal other edge with glue. (Similar process works with fabric—you will want to turn under the open edges of fabric if it is likely to fray.)

To decorate: draw emblems or write Scripture quotations; or draw emblems on white contact paper and color, then cut out, peel, and stick on. For fabric covered derders, you may wish to embroider (thread or liquid) before rolling tube, but with paper it is probably better to wait until tube is covered, so you have a sense of what will show on the rounded surfaces. Punch two holes near one end and tie brightly colored ribbon through; or tie ribbons around derder in two or three places.

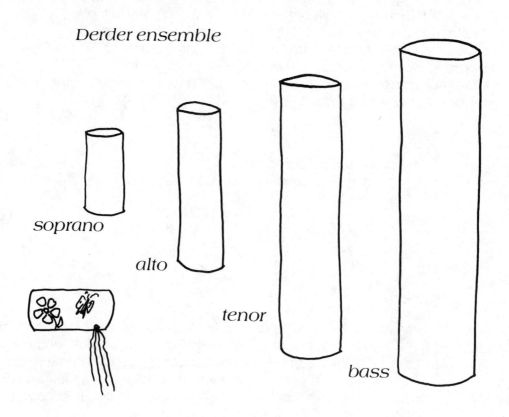

Derder ensemble

soprano

alto

tenor

bass

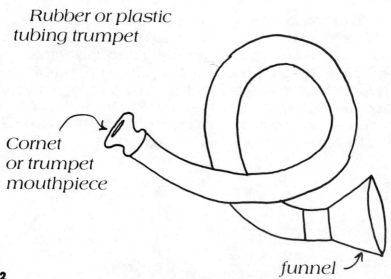

Rubber or plastic
tubing trumpet

Cornet
or trumpet
mouthpiece

funnel

Tambourines

Tambourine is another name for timbrel, and is a rhythm instrument. In addition to the tambourines shown, make shakers and rattles from dried gourds (when they have dried for several months the seeds will rattle inside; paint, wax or decoupage them); tennis ball or orange juice cans with about ¼ cup dried beans, popcorn, or stones inside, decorated and lid taped back on with wide fabric or plastic tape; sticks with small jingle bells attached by ribbon or yarn—or anything that leaps to your eye.

Materials:

Two paper plates or bowls or two foil or aluminum pie pans.
White glue
Scissors or paper punch
Yarn or ribbon for streamers around edge
Marking pens or crayons ro decorate paper plates; paint, if desired, for foil pans.
¼ cup stones, beans, popcorn, rice, or dry macaroni

Instructions:

Decorate outsides of plates (or let child decorate).

Put dried beans or other noisemaking material in plate.

Run a line of glue around edge of plate; place second plate on top and hold in place until glue sets (allow about ½ hour for final drying time).

Punch holes around edge, evenly spaced; tie streamers through holes.

An even simpler tambourine is made from a plastic coffee can lid, at least 5" in diameter. Punch holes around edge; use pipe cleaners cut in half to attach small bells (5–7 bells).

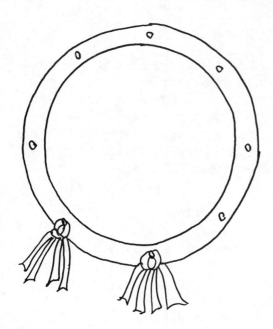

*Two-plate
tambourine*

*Plastic lid
tambourine*

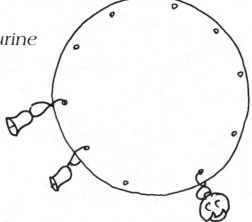

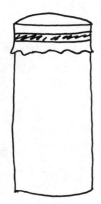

*Shaker—fill
with stones or
dried beans*

VIII. For the Christian Year

"These are my
solemn festivals."

Leviticus 23:2

GIFTS AROUND THE CHRISTIAN YEAR

Advent:

   Advent wreath, Jesse Tree

Christmas:

   Ornaments, Christmas tree skirt, foods, toys

Epiphany:

   Gifts of light; "gold, frankincense and myrrh"—jewelry; incense or potpourri, pomander balls; ointment or lotion (mineral oil with a few drops of lavender or patchouli oil added)

Lent:

   Gifts of time and service; Lenten calendar; earthenware dishes or cups; "fasting foods"—rice, lentils, fish, unleavened bread

Easter:

   Seeds, plants, gardening tools; plastic hosiery eggs with Easter symbol decal, filled with packets of herbs and spices or seeds; natural eggs: boil eggs with outer skins of onions

Pentecost:

   Bibles, Bible story books or coloring books; baskets of early fruits or vegetables; T-shirts and shorts for youngsters

CALENDARS

Make a calendar marking the dates significant to Christians as a helpful balance to the publicity urged on us by the secular marketplace. The fixed dates common to Western Christians are as follows:

Advent—December 1–24 (some include the last Sunday in November)

Christmas—December 25

Epiphany—first Sunday in January after the Octave Day of Christmas

Easter varies from year to year, and its date determines the dates of Ash Wednesday, the Lenten season, and Passion Week, including Palm Sunday, Maundy or Holy Thursday, Good Friday, Holy Saturday.

Pentecost or Whitsunday is seven weeks after Easter.

Some denominations celebrate saints' days and other special feasts; most Christians prefer to make Thanksgiving a religious celebration. Halloween, or All Hallows' Eve, is still a religious festival in some parts of the world, and some families might wish to discover the ancient customs and traditions surrounding this holiday.

Materials:

8½" by 11" paper—
52 sheets for a week-at-a-time calendar
12 sheets for a month-at-a-time calendar
Ruler, sharp pencil
Pen and ink, felt-tip markers, watercolors, or cut-out pictures for decoration. Contact paper or pre-gummed labels make suitable stick-on decorations—draw or color on them with permanent markers for best results.

Instructions:

Measure ½" from either end of paper, and draw a light pencil line; measure $\frac{5}{16}$" from each long side and draw lines.

Place ruler crosswise of paper, with end against one margin line. Make a light dot every 1 $\frac{1}{8}$". Repeat in two or three other places. Turn ruler lengthwise and join dots to make seven lines running the length of the paper between margins.

With ruler end against one end margin and lying along one of the lines you have just drawn, mark off 2" intervals. Repeat along one or two other lines. Turn crosswise and join dots to make four lines running across the paper.

You now have a sheet marked into 35 squares, suitable for one month's dates. Depending on the day of the week which is the first of the month, use extra squares for the name of the month, a decoration, and a quotation if you wish.

Number the dates, add emblems as you wish, color.

Calendar may be placed in a report folder or punched and held together with notebook rings (available at variety stores), ribbon, or yarn. If the calendar may have rough use, put reinforcements over punched holes.

WEEKLY CALENDAR:

Leave $\frac{1}{4}$" margins on long sides of paper. Place end of ruler on one margin and mark every 2"; repeat two or three more times. Draw 3 vertical lines.

With end of ruler against end of paper, mark $\frac{1}{4}$" or $\frac{1}{2}$" margins. Mark center of paper (5$\frac{1}{2}$" from end) in two or three places. Draw line across paper.

You now have eight squares. Use one for month name and any decoration you desire. Mark the date and day of the week in each of the other squares, add emblems or quotations. Punch holes in sides or end, depending on whether your calendar is vertical or horizontal; join as above.

Any relatively stiff paper is suitable for calendars. You may wish to use colored paper (cover stock or colored mimeograph paper, available in office supply stores, is better than construction paper). The ancient Church designated certain colors for its seasons, and you may wish to follow the color scheme in your calendar.

Advent and Lent: purple, dark blue, or off white
Christmas, Epiphany, Easter: white or gold
Pentecost or Whitsunday: red

"Ordinary time"—between Epiphany and Lent in some churches; from Pentecost to the beginning of Advent: green or rose.

The Christian year is divided into festival and non-festival seasons, the "ordinary time" or days of the Lord. Basically, the festival seasons run from Advent through Pentecost, commemorating the preparation for the Messiah, the life, death, resurrection and ascension of Christ, and the descent of the Holy Spirit upon the apostles after the ascension. The season after Pentecost commemorates the life and growth of the Christian community.

another calendar arrangement for 8 1/2 x 11"

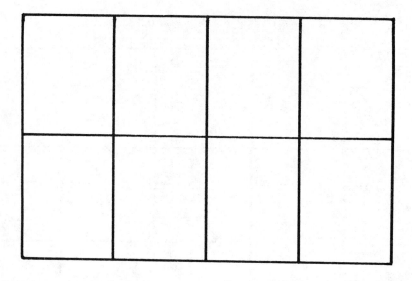

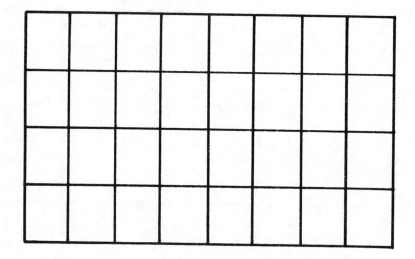

weekly and monthly arrangements
for calendars of 3" x 5" cards

—can be either
vertical or horizontal

ADVENT WREATH

Materials

A metal ring with four candle holders (available at many nurseries or florist shops and at religious supply stores); florist's wire; CANDLES: four purple and one white, or three purple, one pink, and one white. Sets of Advent candles are often available at religious supply stores and some department stores, but do not usually include the white candle. A small single holder for the white candle, which will be placed in the center of the wreath. Assorted cut greens; evergreen cones.

Instructions:

To make the traditional evergreen wreath, cut greens in lengths equaling just less than a fourth the cirumference of the metal ring. Weave between segments of ring, attaching with florist's wire. Continue until wreath is as full as you like it. Attach three or four small evergreen cones, or clusters of tiny fir cones at irregular intervals on the wreath. Place colored candles in four holders on wreath, white candle in center.

A more permanent wreath may be fashioned entirely from evergreen cones. Run florist's wire around each cone near its base, then around metal ring. Attach one at a time. This wreath takes longer to make, but can be packed in tissue paper and kept for years. A few sprigs of fresh greenery and fresh or artificial holly berries will give additional color. Be sure to discard fresh materials each year before storing the wreath.

FAMILY ADVENT WREATH SERVICE

Religious bookstores often sell complete Advent wreath kits, accompanied by leaflets suggesting one or more appropriate ceremonies. Some churches also distribute copies of Advent wreath services to parishioners. Each family may decide to design its own service, depending on the ages of children and the frequency of the celebration (once a day or once a week).

Customarily, the wreath is blessed the Saturday evening before the First Sunday of Advent: the head of the household asks the Lord's blessing on the wreath and on the family as it prepares for the celebration of Christ's coming. Some families then choose to light one candle on the First Sunday of Advent, usually before the evening meal, and an additional one each Sunday thereafter. The candle is left burning during the meal. Other families prefer to light the first candle every evening of the first week of Advent, two every evening the second week, and so on.

The simplest service would consist of a line from Scripture as one member of the family lights the candle or candles, and a prayer—a special prayer on a theme for the week, the Lord's Prayer, or the family's mealtime grace. If the children are very young, you can thus establish the tradition without trying their patience or understanding, and lengthen the service as they grow older.

A longer service might include Scripture readings, two or more prayers, the singing of a hymn, or a discussion about the Old Testament prophecies, the meaning of God's gift, or other themes related to the meaning of Christmas for Christians.

Our own family combines the Advent wreath service with our Advent banner ceremony, using the reading appropriate to the day as well as two or three prayers and our mealtime grace. We light the wreath just before supper; at the end of the meal, before we leave the table, one child moves the family on the banner, then the other blows out the candle.

The candles are sometimes named the "Prophecy Candle," the "Bethlehem Candle," the "Shepherd's Candle," and the "Angel's Candle," the white one in the center being the "Christ Candle." If the pink candle is used, it is sometimes referred to as "Mary's Candle," sometimes as the "Candle of Joy." It is lighted during the third week of Advent, since traditionally the third Sunday was a time of rejoicing in a penitential season. The white candle, if used, is lighted after the other four on Christmas Eve, and by some families again on Christmas morning.

*Advent
wreath
frame*

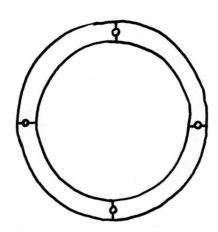

JESSE TREE

"A shoot shall sprout from the stump of Jesse."

(Isaiah 11:1)

"And Jesse was the father of King David."

(Matthew 1:6)

The Jesse Tree commemorates the Old Testament preparation for the coming of the Messiah. There is no "right" set of symbols for the tree, so if you wish to use a real tree with ornaments you may add more every year. Another way to use the tree is to add one ornament each day of Advent.

Materials:

Any well-shaped dead branch, or a piece of driftwood with branches and hollows. Place in a can or tub of sand, making sure the base is stable. An alternative is a lilac branch—the ornaments would need to be lightweight. According to folklore, a lilac branch cut on the first day of Advent and kept in tepid water will blossom on Christmas Day—and, no matter what color the lilac usually is, the blooms will be white.

Ornaments, like Christmas tree ornaments, may be balsa, styrofoam, baker's clay, felt, or stuffed cloth. If the ornaments are not intended to be long-lasting, you may even use lightweight cardboard, posterboard, or paper.

Other versions of the Jesse Tree can be crafted from paper or cloth. Hang a strip of shelf paper on the wall or the front of your refrigerator. Draw a rough trunk and branches from bottom to top, and glue on an emblem each day of Advent (or cut emblems from contact paper and stick on).

A permanent Jesse Tree wall hanging, of felt or other sturdy fabric, may have emblems appliquéd or attached one a day with pins or Velcro.

Dead branch
in sand

Shelf
paper

Banner or hanging

—tree may be embroidered
or appliqued

—emblems may be placed
on trunk as well as
branches

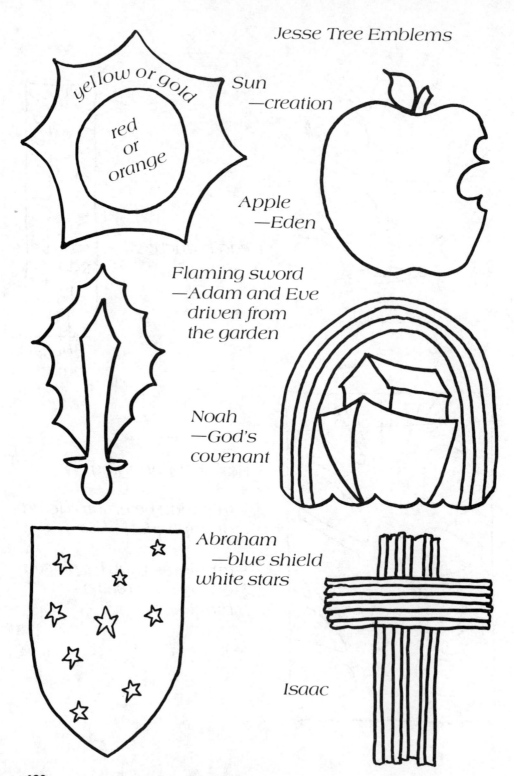

Jesse Tree Emblems

yellow or gold

red
or
orange

Sun
—creation

Apple
—Eden

Flaming sword
—Adam and Eve
driven from
the garden

Noah
—God's
covenant

Abraham
—blue shield
white stars

Isaac

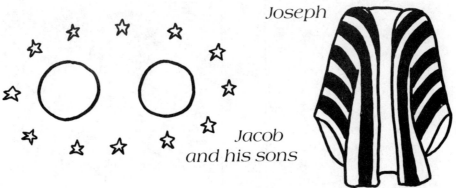

Joseph

Jacob
and his sons

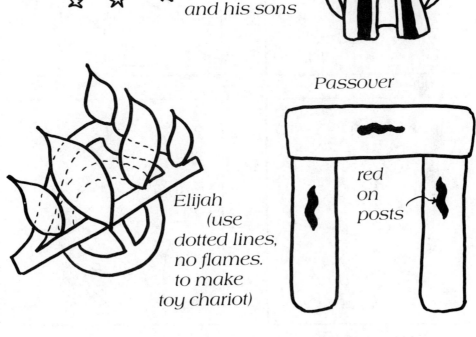

Passover

Elijah
(use
dotted lines,
no flames,
to make
toy chariot)

red
on
posts

Miriam—tambourine

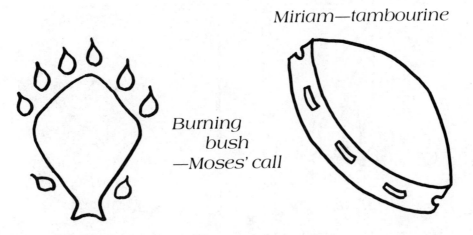

Burning
bush
—Moses' call

129

Christmas motifs

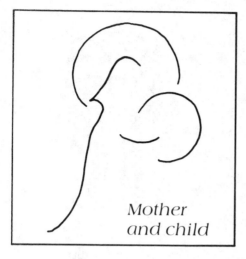

Mother
and child

Angels

Three
Kings

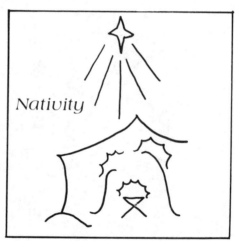

Nativity

Bethlehem

Christmas
rose

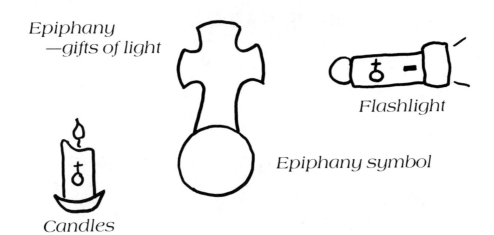

Epiphany
—gifts of light

Candles

Epiphany symbol

Flashlight

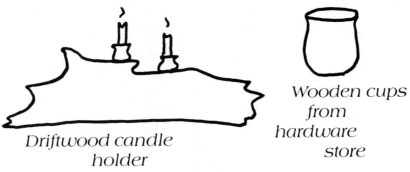

Driftwood candle holder

Wooden cups from hardware store

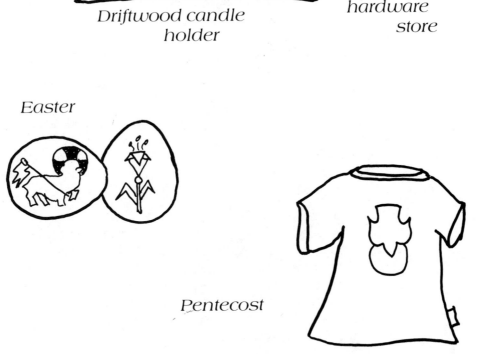

Easter

Pentecost

SCRIPTURE CAKE

*"And thou shalt take fine flour,
and bake twelve cakes thereof."*
(Leviticus 24:5)

The recipe for this cake, also sometimes called "Grandma's Bible Cake," is found, in one form or another, in regional cookbooks or church cookbooks throughout the country, and its origin is traced back through the pioneers to early New England.

Ingredients:

$4\frac{1}{2}$ cups 1 Kings 4:22 (flour)
1 cup Judges 5:25, last clause (butter)
2 cups Jeremiah 6:20 (sugar)
2 cups 1 Samuel 30:12 (raisins)
2 cups Nahum 3:12 (figs)
2 cups Numbers 17:8 (almonds)
2 tablespoons 1 Samuel 14:25 (honey)
1 pinch Leviticus 2:13 (salt)
6 Jeremiah 17:11 (eggs)
$\frac{1}{2}$ cup Judges 4:19 (milk)
Spices, 2 Chronicles 9:9

Scripture says, "a very great quantity of spices." Try the following; or adapt to suit your own taste. You may also take amounts from any equivalent fruitcake recipe in your favorite cookbook.

2 tsp. cinnamon
1 tsp. cloves
1 tsp. allspice
$\frac{1}{4}$ tsp. nutmeg, mace, cardamon

Cream butter and sugar, add flour; chop figs and almonds; beat milk and eggs together. Add all ingredients to flour mixture, and follow Solomon's directions in Proverbs 23:14—"beat him with a rod." Leviticus 26:26—bake—in a greased loaf pan, at 325 degrees, for 50 minutes to an hour. Turn on a rack to cool, wait a few hours to slice easily. This cake is good hot as well as cold.

IX. Time and Service

*"Insofar as you did this
to one of the least of
these brothers of mine,
you did it to me."*

Matthew 25:40

"INASMUCH AS" GIFTS

Materials:

Yourself, your caring, one or more other persons.

Occasionally material goods may be part of the gift, but frequently not.

Gifts of time and service are easy to overlook because often they are (or seem to be) quite small.

Instructions:

Keep your eyes and ears attuned to the needs of others, especially if those needs are unstated.

Try to respond by giving what is *really* needed, rather than a substitute, no matter how costly or showy.

Examples of gifts:

An hour a week or a month reading to someone who is blind or a shut-in.

An hour as often as you can to play a musical instrument or sing with senior citizens, a class of handicapped children, a pediatrics ward, a homebound person, residents of a nursing home, a day care center, a church-school class.

A Saturday morning caring for someone's small children at your home, no strings attached, so parent(s) can shop, clean house, go back to bed, or visit friends.

Write a letter to someone away from home—in the service, or at school.

Teach a class at a correctional facility, a community center, or a recreation department.

Give a day of "respite care" for someone who is housebound caring for an ill or handicapped person.

When you shop for groceries, get something for your local emergency food shelf.

Skip a meal, or a day's worth of meals, and give the cost to a hunger project.

Cook extra, and take a meal to someone who has been taking care of sick kids or who has just plain had a hard week.

Help someone with housekeeping or laundry.

Do a family member's chores (without mentioning it).

Make clothes or blankets for an orphanage.

Help a teenager pick up dropped books.

Get a crying child in the grocery store to smile.

Offer to write letters for someone who is physically unable to do so.

There are many more such gifts. If we are to tithe, or give a tenth of our income, it might be a good idea to think of tithing time as well. Inasmuch as you have done it unto one of the least of these ...

BIBLIOGRAPHY

Alexander, Pat (ed). *Eerdman's Family Encyclopedia of the Bible.* Grand Rapids: Wm. B. Eerdmans Publishing Co., 1978.

The Beautiful Crafts Book. New York: Sterling Publishing Co., Inc., 1976.

Better Homes and Gardens Creative Crafts and Stitchery. Des Moines: Meredith Corp., 1976.

Botsford, Shirley J. *Between Thimble and Thumb.* New York: Holt, Rinehart and Winston, 1979.

Bradshaw-Smith, Gillian. *Adventures in Toy-Making.* New York: Taplinger Publishing Co., 1976.

Caney, Steven. *Steven Caney's Kids' America.* New York: Workman Publishing Co., 1978.

Fiarotta, Phyllis. *Phyllis Fiarotta's Nostalgia Crafts Book.* New York: Workman Publishing Co., 1974.

Heyer, Robert (ed.). *Celebrating Advent.* New York: Paulist Press, 1975.

Hunter, Ilene, and Marilyn Judson. *Simple Folk Instruments To Make and Play.* New York: Simon and Schuster, 1977.

Hynes, Arleen. *The Passover Meal: A Ritual for Christian Homes.* New York: Paulist Press, 1972.

Mills, Sonya (ed.). *The Book of Presents.* New York: Pantheon Books, 1979.

Neubecker, Ottfried. *Heraldry: Sources, Symbols and Meaning. New York: McGraw-Hill, 1976.*

O'Neill, Jeanne Lamb. *The Make-It-Merry Christmas Book.* New York: William Morrow & Co., 1977.

Post, W. Ellwood, *Saints, Signs and Symbols.* New York: Morehouse-Barlow Co., 1962, 1974.

Rosenberg, Sharon and Joan Wiener. *The Illustrated Hassle-Free Make Your Own Clothes Book.* New York: Bantam, 1972.

Ryan, Pat and Rosemary. *Lent Begins at Home: Family Prayers and Activities.* Liguori: Liguori Publications, 1978.

Sorkin, Gerri. *Keepsake Transfer Collection.* Berkeley: Craftways, 1980.

Tangerman, E.J. *Whittling and Woodcarving.* New York: Dover Publications, Inc., 1962.

Torre, Frank D. *It's Easy To Carve.* Garden City: Doubleday, 1977.

Travnikar, Rock, O.F.M. *The Blessing Cup.* New York: St. Anthony Messenger Press, 1979.

Walther, Tom. *Make Mine Music!* Boston: Little, Brown & Co., 1981.

Weidmann, Carl F. (ed.). *A Dictionary of Church Terms and Symbols.*
    Norwalk: C.R. Gibson Co., 1974.
Westland, Pamela, and Paula Critchley. *The Art of Dried and Pressed
    Flowers.* New York: Crown Publishers, Inc., 1974.
Wilson, Erica. *Erica Wilson's Christmas World.* New York: Charles
    Scribner's Sons, 1980.

Ann Schweninger

Christmas Secrets

·FATHER·

·BUTTERCUP·

·BUTTON BROWN·

·MOTHER·

·DAISY·

Puffin Books

PUFFIN BOOKS
Viking Penguin Inc., 40 West 23rd Street, New York, New York 10010, U.S.A.
Penguin Books Ltd, Harmondsworth, Middlesex, England
Penguin Books Australia Ltd, Ringwood, Victoria, Australia
Penguin Books Canada Limited, 2801 John Street, Markham, Ontario, Canada L3R 1B4
Penguin Books (N.Z.) Ltd, 182–190 Wairau Road, Auckland 10, New Zealand

First published by Viking Penguin Inc. 1984
Published in Picture Puffins 1986
Copyright © Ann Schweninger, 1984
All rights reserved
Printed in Japan by Dai Nippon Printing Co. Ltd.
Set in Windsor

Library of Congress Cataloging in Publication Data
Schweninger, Ann.   Christmas secrets.
Summary: The Rabbit children's Christmas prepa-
rations include building a mystery snowman, writing
letters to Santa, and baking Christmas cookies.
[1. Christmas—Fiction.   2. Rabbits—Fiction]   I. Title.
PZ7.S41263Ch   1986   [E]   86-3249   ISBN 0-14-050577-6

For Ron

The Snowman

The Letter

Christmas Eve

WHAAA!

NOW LET'S MAKE THREE SPECIAL ONES.